D0975613

OCEANSIDE PUBLIC LIBRARY

3 1232 00321 3636

VIRGINIA WOOLF

A Study of the Short Fiction

Also Available in Twayne's Studies in Short Fiction Series

Twayne's Studies in Short Fiction

Gordon Weaver, General Editor
Oklahoma State University

VIRGINIA WOOLF
Photograph courtesy of the Wesleyan University Library

VIRGINIA WOOLF

A Study of the Short Fiction

Dean R. Baldwin

The Pennsylvania State University at Erie,
The Behrend College

TWAYNE PUBLISHERS • BOSTON
A Division of G. K. Hall & Co.

Copyright © 1989 by G. K. Hall & Co.
All rights reserved.
Published by Twayne Publishers
A division of G. K. Hall & Co.
70 Lincoln Street, Boston, Massachusetts 02111

Twayne's Studies in Short Fiction Series No. 6

Copyediting supervised by Barbara Sutton.
Book design and production by Janet Z. Reynolds.
Typeset in 10/12 Caslon by Compset, Inc.

Printed on permanent/durable acid-free paper
and bound in the United States of America.

Library of Congress Cataloging-in-Publication Data

Baldwin, Dean R., 1942–
    Virginia Woolf : a study of the short fiction.

    (Twayne's studies in short fiction ; no 6)
    Bibliography: p.
    Includes index.
    1. Woolf, Virginia, 1882–1941—Criticism and interpretation.
    2. Short story.   I. Title.   II. Series.
PR6045.072Z542   1989   823'.912   88-34765
ISBN 0-8057-8314-8 (alk. paper)

For my wife, Vicki,
with all my love.

Contents

Preface

Virginia Woolf is almost universally regarded as an imposing and formidable presence in the modern British novel. After a period of relative decline in the 1940s and 1950s, her reputation has grown steadily among scholars in the last decades, resulting in an outpouring of critical books and articles about her work, together with an imposing number of biographies and studies of her Bloomsbury friends and milieu. To most ordinary readers, she is a "difficult" novelist, an author whose works are second in complexity only to those of James Joyce.

It is somewhat surprising, therefore, to learn that her short stories have been relatively little studied. The bibliography at the end of this volume lists only a handful of articles devoted to her short fiction, whereas a complete bibliography of studies about her and her novels fills a substantial volume. This is the first book-length survey of her stories.

The aim of the present study is to present an overview of all her work in short fiction. Since Virginia Woolf experimented continually with the short story form, sometimes writing stories that seem more like essays, at other times stories that approach the lyric poem, critics may legitimately argue over which of her prose pieces are in fact stories. Rather than engage in this argument, I have decided to accept as short stories all of the works included in Susan Dick's edition, *The Complete Shorter Fiction of Virginia Woolf*. This edition, the most complete and reliable guide to Virginia Woolf's stories, provides a convenient and authoritative textual basis for this study. Since this book is aimed primarily at students, teachers, and general readers rather than at scholars, it makes no attempt to address the thornier issues of Woolfian criticism, and it consciously avoids adopting any of the currently fashionable critical approaches.

Writing in her essay on George Moore in *The Death of the Moth*, Virginia Woolf noted, "Are not all novels about the writer's self . . . ? It is only as he sees people that we can see them; his fortunes colour and his oddities shape his vision until what we see is not the thing itself, but the thing seen and the seer inextricably mixed" (*Collected Essays*,

338). Not only this isolated quotation but also the work of other biographers and critics, plus my own reading of Woolf's diaries and letters, embolden me to take a chronological and biographical approach to these stories. What this study attempts to do is to see Virginia Woolf's short stories as growing out of particular times and pressures in her life. Still, I have tried to follow this approach pragmatically rather than slavishly and to draw biographical connections only when these can be supported by documented incidents or by clear passages from the diaries or letters. I have made no attempt to psychoanalyze the author, preferring to leave that to more qualified scholars.

The biographical bias of the study means that it was most convenient to consider the stories chronologically. This I have done to the extent that the evidence permits dating the stories, but I have deviated from strict chronology on occasion when other considerations seemed more compelling. The combination of biographical criticism and chronological overview should provide students of Virginia Woolf's short fiction with a sense of how her art developed and matured over time, even though it may obscure some of the thematic or technical links among the stories.

The other theme of this essay is experimentalism. Virginia Woolf was an innovator in the novel and essay, and she is no less original in her short stories. In fact, it is chiefly as an experimenter that she is valued by the anthologists. Unfortunately, she left few direct statements about her theory of the short story; there are no manifestos like "Modern Fiction" or "Mr. Bennett and Mrs. Brown" regarding the short story. Comments about her experiments in short fiction, therefore, must be related to her pronouncements about the novel and to what can be inferred from the stories themselves. This means that her exact aims in a particular story or kind of story must always be to some extent conjectural. In particular, one would like to know why in her later stories she turned to traditional techniques and devices after a lifetime of restless experimentation, but the evidence is indirect and hence inconclusive. Nevertheless, tracing her various approaches to the genre is an important aspect of this study, an aspect, incidentally, compatible with and even complementary to, the biographical element.

Assessing the literary importance of these stories is a complicated task, not least because of Woolf's towering reputation as a novelist. Her place in literary history will ultimately depend almost entirely on the novels, with the stories providing interesting sidelights. But this is more a statement about the prejudices of historians and critics than about the intrinsic merits of the stories, for there is no doubt that her achievement in short fiction is considerable. Nevertheless, stating the basis of her achievement is not easy, in part because her stories are so various and individual; she neither followed a school of short story writing nor founded one.

From this distance, however, it seems probable that "The Mark on the Wall" and "Kew Gardens" will remain important for their technical and stylistic innovations, whereas "An Unwritten Novel," "Moments of Being: Slater's Pins Have No Points," and "The Lady in a Looking Glass" will continue to arouse interest because of their handling of point of view. "The New Dress," "The Introduction," and "The Man Who Loved His Kind" will be valued for thematic reasons as well as for their excellent writing, whereas "Lappin and Lapinova" or "The Shooting Party" may continue to interest readers because they are quite traditional in technique.

In other words, Woolf's stories exemplify an astonishing variety of excellence, a fact that may ultimately work against her reputation as a story writer. It is easier for the anthologist, historian, or critic to deal with a writer who can be neatly classified than to discuss one who defies categorizing. In the best of all possible worlds, Woolf would be remembered for the full range of her story writing, for the vigor and flexibility of her style, the suggestive power of her invention, and the acuity of her psychological portraits. Perhaps, paradoxically, the range of her achievement in the novel will foster a similar admiration for her short fiction.

The critical writings collected at the end of this volume testify to the quality and depth of Woolf's short fiction as well as to the variety of critical approaches her work accommodates. These essays have been selected for their intrinsic value, of course, but also because preference was given to complete essays that shed light on a major story or on a variety of stories. As yet, no definitive study of Woolf's short fiction has appeared to focus and unify the critical process. Given the variety of Woolf's stories, such a study may be unlikely. Nevertheless, Virginia Woolf has stimulated and will continue to stimulate a lively debate about the meaning and value of her work. Her reputation as a novelist seems secure; her reputation as a short story writer is still emerging.

A word of explanation on my handling of quotations from the diaries and letters is in order. In both her diaries and letters, Virginia Woolf often paid little attention to the niceties of grammar and spelling, and of course she alluded to contemporary people and events without explaining them. The editors of her diaries, Anne Olivier Bell, and of her letters, Nigel Nicolson and Joanne Trautmann, expanded her abbreviations and explained allusions as necessary but left her erratic spelling and frequent abbreviations untouched. When quoting from the letters or diaries, I have followed their example, leaving obvious errors in spelling and punctuation uncorrected and unsullied by the use of *sic*. On occasion, however, I have had to supply identifications of persons or events not provided by the editors. To distinguish these from their additions in square brackets [ ], I have used the mark { } to indicate my own additions, clarifications, and explanations. I trust these will assist the reader without unduly cluttering the text.

In conclusion I wish to thank all those whose support made this work possible. In particular, I wish to thank Harcourt Brace Jovanovich for permission to quote from the stories, diaries, and letters, and to the various journals that allowed me to reprint their articles. On a more personal level, I am indebted to Behrend College for its support of my research, to Mrs. Norma Hartner for her expert typing and word processing, to Prof. Edward Hungerford for his corrections and suggestions, and above all to my long-suffering wife for her unfailing love and support, without which this book could not have been written.

Dean R. Baldwin

*The Pennsylvania State University
at Erie, The Behrend College*

Acknowledgments

The author wishes to thank the following individuals and institutions for granting permission to quote the material that made this book possible.

Harcourt Brace Jovanovich, Inc., for permission to quote passages from *The Complete Shorter Fiction of Virginia Woolf*, edited by Susan Dick, copyright © 1985 by Quentin Bell and Angelica Garnett. Harcourt Brace Jovanovich, Inc., for permission to quote excerpts from *The Letters of Virginia Woolf*, edited by Nigel Nicolson and Joanne Trautmann, copyright © 1980, 1979, 1977, 1976 by Quentin Bell and Angelica Garnett. Harcourt Brace Jovanovich for permission to quote from *The Diary of Virginia Woolf*, vols. 1–5, edited by Anne Olivier Bell, copyright © 1984, 1982, 1980, 1978, 1977 by Quentin Bell and Angelica Garnett. Harcourt Brace Jovanovich for permission to reprint "Mr. Bennett and Mrs. Brown" from *The Captain's Deathbed and Other Essays* by Virginia Woolf, copyright 1950, 1978 by Harcourt Brace Jovanovich. Harcourt Brace Jovanovich for permission to reprint "Modern Fiction" from *The Common Reader* by Virginia Woolf, copyright 1925 by Harcourt Brace Jovanovich, Inc.; renewed 1953 by Leonard Woolf.

Part 1

THE SHORT FICTION:
A CRITICAL ANALYSIS

Experience and Experiment in the Short Stories of Virginia Woolf

If writers of fiction can be divided roughly into two classes—those who excel at the novel and those whose reputation rests on short stories—then Virginia Woolf would have to be considered primarily as a novelist. What she achieved in the remarkable series of books beginning with *Jacob's Room* and extending through her posthumous novel *Between the Acts* is now recognized as among the great contributions to fiction of this century. Unlike her contemporary James Joyce (one of the few notable exceptions to the generalization offered above), Virginia Woolf has not been highly regarded for her short stories. Most biographies and critical works focus almost exclusively on the novels, and, although essays on individual stories are increasingly common, no comprehensive study has yet been done on her short fiction.

To some extent, therefore, it is proper to say that Woolf's short stories have been neglected by critics in favor of her justly admired novels. Woolf herself doubtless contributed to this situation by publishing relatively few stories in her lifetime and by devoting very little of her analytical and critical energy to discussing the form. She espoused no theory of short fiction and seldom mentioned her stories at any length in her diaries or letters. Nevertheless, the work of genius always repays study, and the meticulous revisions of the stories she did publish, not to mention her ambivalent but often jealous attitude toward Katherine Mansfield, suggest that she invested a great deal of creative energy in the stories she finished. Moreover, even a cursory reading of her short fiction reveals a restless experimentation with form and technique that frequently parallels and illuminates the longer works.

This study considers the extent to which events in the writer's life and currents in her thought permeated the stories as they did the novels, a feature that gives the stories added interest to students of Woolf's life and art. There is little danger that the stories will overshadow the novels in importance, but as Virginia Woolf's reputation continues to rise, her stories take an additional interest as works valuable to consider in their own right—as a growing body of criticism attests.

In his survey of the eighteen stories published in *Monday or Tuesday* (1921) and *The Haunted House* (1944), Jean Guiguet identifies three periods during which Virginia Woolf actively engaged in story writing: 1917–21, 1927–29, and 1938–40.[1] This scheme ignores the very earliest attempts of 1906–09 and the posthumous stories collected by Susan Dick, which were written at various times throughout Virginia Woolf's career.[2] Hence, Guiguet's divisions should be amended to 1917–21, 1923–29, and 1938–41.

During the first period defined by Guiguet, Woolf was searching for fictional techniques to express new vision and, like many authors, chose the shorter form as her medium. Not surprisingly, this is her most original and experimental period, when in her two most famous stories, "The Mark on the Wall" (1917) and "Kew Gardens" (1919), she pushed the story form to its limits. Others of this period in the experimental vein include "A Haunted House," "Monday or Tuesday," and the meditation "Blue and Green," all published in 1921.

The second period, 1923–29, includes all the stories gathered in Stella McNichol's collection of Mrs. Dalloway stories,[3] down to "Mrs. Dalloway in Bond Street" (1923). These stories subject the form to less pressure than the earlier ones, although Woolf is obviously using the shorter form to explore themes and techniques of character presentation, dialogue, and construction that would also appear in *Mrs. Dalloway* (1925), *To the Lighthouse* (1927), and *The Waves* (1931). There then follows a rather long fallow interval during which Woolf apparently only tinkered with short fiction. The satirical "Scenes from the Life of a British Naval Officer" (1931?) and the obviously rough "Ode Written Partly in Prose on Seeing the Name of Cutbush Above a Butcher's Shop" (1934) belong to this period.

The last period, 1938–41, contains some of Woolf's most interesting and yet conventional short fiction, paralleling her development in later novels like *The Years* (1937). In "The Duchess and the Jeweller" (1938), "Gipsy, the Mongrel" (1939), and "The Legacy" (1940), for example, Woolf relies on plot, incident, and conventional devices of characterization and description in ways that early in her career she rejected and criticized. To some extent, these stories reflect the fact that they were commissioned by high-paying American magazines, for by this time Woolf was more than happy to oblige editors and readers with stories of the type they were used to reading if the fee were sufficient. This is not to suggest that she "sold out" to popular taste, but she did adopt a pragmatic approach at least to marketing her material, and in any event the conventionality of these later stories seems consistent with her artistic temperament at the time. One of the subthemes of the discussion to follow will be this change in Woolf's approach to short fiction over time.

"Experimentalism" in Woolf's short fiction will, therefore, be an important part of the following discussion, suggesting that the term itself needs clarification. A literary experiment is roughly analogous to a scientific one in that it proceeds from some hypothesis about what fiction can and cannot do, or should and should not do. It then tests that hypothesis by trial and error and compares the results to what the hypothesis predicted. If the experiment succeeds, some new insight is gained into the possibilities of language to order and describe the universe; if it fails, new trials may be necessary or the hypothesis may have to be abandoned. This sort of comparison cannot be pushed too far, of course, since in science Nature is the ultimate arbiter, whereas in literature aesthetic considerations are paramount. In the first part of Virginia Woolf's career, she seems concerned primarily but not exclusively with epistemology—how we know what we know. Thus, the theme of her stories from this period is often the question of knowing or understanding. It is essentially on this ground that she challenges the "materialism" of Wells, Bennett, and Galsworthy in her essay "Modern Fiction" (1919); true knowledge resides in the interior of the narrator and her subject, not in the external details of life. Her stories seek ways to explore this interior, in part through new uses of language, in part by employing a new literary psychology, reflected in point of view.

In the second period, 1923–29, her experiments do not so much change as focus on the problem of knowing and revealing character. Language is tamer, less exuberant, the imagery less daring in these stories; but her sentences are often long, complex, and carefully modulated in rhythm and meaning. The manifesto for this period is "Mr. Bennett and Mrs. Brown" (1924), which discusses at length the problems of delineating character, using as an example a fictitious Mrs. Brown, whom Woolf imagines seated opposite her in a railway carriage. The hypothesis enunciated in the essay and tested in the stories is the extent to which we can know and create literary characters by techniques lying somewhere between traditional interior monologue and "stream of consciousness."

There is a second sense of the term "experiment" in literature that differs entirely from the way the term is used in science. For a given author, any movement into previously untried territory may be considered an experiment, even though other authors have pioneered the approach or technique. It is primarily in this sense that Virginia Woolf experiments during the third phase of her short fiction career. Having pushed her own methods to the limit, she turns at last to conventional devices of plot and point of view, and in response her style moderates as well. Sentences are shorter and less complex; vocabulary and imagery are plainer and less daring. Perhaps because the style and techniques are largely conventional, there is no corollary in this period to the theoretical essays of the previous decade. Nevertheless, it is still true to say that Woolf continued to experiment with short story form until the very end.

Biography is an often maligned and sometimes abused critical tool. Used clumsily, it can become a substitute for criticism or an excuse for idle speculation. The wealth of documentary material contained in Woolf's diaries and letters has yielded valuable information about the novels, and there is no reason to suppose that it has any less relevance to the short stories. Because the evidence is abundant and often unequivocal, these sources can confidently be used to illuminate the origin, content, and sometimes the meaning of the stories. The diaries and letters also help to place the stories in context and, perhaps more important, aid in humanizing their author. To see in an early story like "Phyllis and Rosamond" (1906) a young woman's fears about her future or in a later story like "Lappin and Lapinova" (1938) a mature woman's commentary on her own marriage is to read these stories in a fresh new light. Biography is a valid critical tool, and in the study of these short stories it has the additional advantage of providing a convenient organizational device by which to trace Virginia Woolf's experiments.

These two themes—Virginia Woolf's restless experimentation in short story form and technique, and the relationship of these stories to her own life—will constitute the twin vantage points for this survey of her short fiction. It is hoped that these will prove illuminating in themselves and suggestive of other ideas and approaches, for Virginia Woolf's stories, like her novels, are a rich body of fiction that will amply reward the careful and critical reader.

Tradition and an Individual Talent

The biographical element visible throughout Virginia Woolf's short fiction is present from the earliest surviving story, "Phyllis and Rosamond" (1906). Here, Phyllis (age twenty-eight) and her younger sister Rosamond (twenty-four) are almost certainly aspects of Vanessa and Virginia Stephen at an earlier period when half-brother George Duckworth attempted to turn the reluctant sisters into respectable socialites. Even twenty years after this story Virginia confided to her diary, "The heat has come, bringing with it the inexplicably disagreeable memories of parties, & George Duckworth; a fear haunts me even now, as I drive past Park Lane on top of a bus, & think of Lady Arthur Russell & so on."[4] The result in Virginia was a lifelong horror of certain kinds of parties and social situations.

Phyllis and Rosamond, however, are less rebellious than were Vanessa and Virginia: they tamely submit to their mother's tedious analysis of their "performance" on a given night, and although they chafe at the prospect of having to marry dull young men of their class, they accept the eventuality as inevitable. An incident that confirms their fears occurs when they attend a "bohemian" party at the Tristrams' Bloomsbury residence and encounter sophisticated discussions of art and music as well as shockingly advanced views about women, sex, and marriage. Retreating to the comfortable familiarity of home, they realize that they are incapable of transcending middle-class conventions. This aspect of the story is particularly interesting because it represents the life that Vanessa and Virginia escaped when their father died in 1904 and they scandalized their relations by moving from Hyde Park Place and setting up a home of their own in Bloomsbury. The Tristrams, therefore, are the freedom-loving aspects of the two sisters, and what the story dramatizes is the tension the young Stephen women faced at this crucial stage of their careers. Phyllis and Rosamond are what Vanessa and Virginia might have become.

Apart from its biographical interest, "Phyllis and Rosamond" indicates Virginia Woolf's early concern with feminist issues. The narrator notes with some sarcasm early in the story that writing about young women rather than young men is unusual. She believes, however, that her portrait of these ordinary young women "may possibly have some value" (17). Phyllis and Rosamond represent their class, young women with some accomplishments but no real education, of intelligence and sensibility but no way to express or pursue them in a male-dominated culture. They have neither the courage nor the talent to break free of the role society has assigned them, and thus when they "choose" to return to conventional life, they do so of necessity.

"The Mysterious Case of Miss V.," written at about the same time, takes up a similar theme with an elderly woman as the central figure. Miss V. (the initial is significant) is an "invisible woman," one of the multitudes of London's elderly spinsters and widows who swell the ranks at exhibits, concerts, and recitals without being noticed. She is not a presence or personality, but a "grey shadow" (31), an image recalling passages from the previous story describing women as those who "cluster in the shade" and dance like marionettes in "partial light" (17). When the narrator senses vaguely that something is missing from the concerts, it is some time before she realizes with a start that the something is Miss V. The story ends melodramatically when the narrator rushes to the house of Miss V. only to discover that she died the day before. The predictable conclusion mars the story, but its tone and narrative stance look forward to later, more controlled stories in which the unspoken relations between narrator and subject are exploited for greater effect. The name of the central character, Miss V., suggests that the young author is thinking of herself, Miss Virginia, projected forty years into the future. This is the other horn of the marriage dilemma, the way she may end up if she does not find a husband. These two early stories, therefore, may be interpreted as fictional workings out of the author's concerns about what the future holds for her as a woman, and hence for young women generally. She may choose between marriage to a shallow and trite man of her class or spinsterhood, with no more identity than an initial and no more substance—socially at least—than a shadow.

"The Journal of Mistress Joan Martyn" continues the young writer's exploration of women's shadowy place in history and society by presenting the diary of a young medieval woman within the framing tale of a contemporary female historian who relies on a controversial mix of fact and fiction in writing her accounts of the past. This narrator, Rosamond Merridew, is the author's mouthpiece—the name Rosamond being used for the second time in three stories is surely not mere coincidence. She articulates two ideas of history that Virginia Woolf expounded throughout her life: that history as conceived and written by men places too much emphasis on statesmen and generals and too little on the lives of ordinary people and that facts unillumined by imagination are of limited value. The modern frame tale holding the medieval diary narrative is a good device for emphasizing the contrasts the author wishes to stress: the obscurity of women versus the prominence of men; the difference between history and herstory, neatly epitomized by the owner of the diary, Mr. Martyn, who regards the medieval narrative as less important than the farm's stud books; the civilizing and ordering role of women as against the chaos of war and pillage instigated by men; and the "triviality" of Joan's daily life in comparison to the exciting adventures of poetry brought to her by the wandering minstrel.

The story's themes and their relation to Virginia Woolf's other works have been ably analyzed by Louise A. DeSalvo,[5] and indeed it is in its thematic and structural elements that the story is most effective. It is, of course, unfinished, in that it was not published during Woolf's lifetime and hence did not receive her usual rigorous rewriting and revising. This unfinished state is most clearly evident in the fictional diary, where, in spite of Virginia Stephen's familiarity with Middle English and medieval history, neither the language nor many of the attitudes ring true. Probably she was wise not to attempt to cast the diary into pseudo–fifteenth-century language, but the style and vocabulary are too obviously modern to be convincing: "There comes a week, or maybe it is only a day, when the year seems poised consciously on its topmost peak; it stays there motionless for a long or a short time, as though in majestic contemplation, and then slowly sinks like a monarch descending from his throne, and wraps itself round in darkness" (57). These are hardly the musings of a home-tutored diarist—male or female—of any century before the nineteenth. Similarly, the literate minstrel with his pack of illuminated books (unless we are to assume that he pillaged them from some manorial or monastic library) seems highly unlikely. The point is not that Virginia Stephen made occasional errors in historical language or fact, but that the medieval narrative shows too many signs of contrivance for its thematic purpose. Details of Joan Martyn's daily life, her musings on men and war, and her thoughts on marriage and social class are too self-conscious and calculating. Careful revision might have been able to remove these defects without losing the important points. As the story stands, it is most interesting as an experiment in narrative technique and as an indication of Woolf's early commitment to ideas that would find more powerful expression in *A Room of One's Own, Anon.*, and *Three Guineas.*

Although these stories show definite thematic links to her later work, they differ markedly in technique and style from Woolf's mature short fiction. The authorial voice is quaintly nineteenth century with a clubby, arm-around-the shoulder quality in the omniscient narrator. "Phyllis and Rosamond" begins, "In this very curious age, when we are beginning to require pictures of people, their minds and their coats, a faithful outline, drawn with no skill but veracity, may possibly have some value" (17), and "Miss V." sounds much like it: "It is a commonplace that there is no loneliness like that of one who finds himself alone in a crowd" (30). Miss Merridew, the narrator of "The Journal," strikes a similar attitude.

In diction, tone, and approach, these stories sound like the work of Bennett or Galsworthy rather than that of Virginia Woolf. Techniques of character building, indeed the whole approach to character, are equally conservative. The author describes the externals, probes the thoughts, interprets the actions, and records the conversations of her creations with an almost patronizing certainty, guiding the reader by the elbow through the narrative. The dialogue is formal; descriptions and analyses are prim, bordering on the smug. In spite of the strong emotions and convictions behind the stories, their surface belongs to a settled Victorianism. There are few traces of the restless intellect and wavering uncertainty of middle and later works. These stories, like *The Voyage Out* (1915), are exercises in traditional methods, not explorations or new approaches.

"Memoirs of a Novelist" appears in hindsight as the harbinger of new directions in Virginia Woolf's fiction. Its techniques and style are still largely conventional, but she extends herself by casting the story as a review article assessing Miss Linsett's vapid biography of an author of trivial romances, Miss Willatt. The review article form, however, is stretched to its limits by the author's imaginative musings on both of these women. The story thus has three layers: the "real" Miss Willatt, Miss Willatt as portrayed by her biographer, and the narrator's observations and speculations on these two Victorian women. This story reflects, like her early reviews, Virginia Woolf's misgivings about biography as it is usually written and, by extension, of realistic fiction and its conventions and trappings. "What right has the world to know

about men and women? What can a biographer tell it?" (63)—the narrator asks and then reflects on these questions in a way that casts doubt
not only on the inept work of Miss Linsett but also on the value of
"fact" itself. Miss Linsett's ineptitudes stem partly from a failure of
imagination, as when she glosses over Miss Willatt's first ball and fails
to see how miserably out of place the plain young woman must have
felt. In the end, the author despairs of learning anything from Miss
Linsett and takes on herself the task of assessing Miss Willatt's
character.

Miss Linsett's failures as a biographer are paralleled by Miss Willatt's
as a novelist: "Miss Willatt adopted the theory that no training is necessary, but thought it indecent to describe what she had seen, so that
instead of a portrait of her brothers (and one had led a very queer life)
or a memory of her father (for which we should have been grateful) she
invented Arabian lovers and set them on the banks of the Orinoco"
(69). Deception and denial of reality thus became prominent features
of Miss Willatt's character, and in later years she claimed to be a sort
of Sibyl, surrounded by Miss Linsett and other women who needed
"to be told that they were parts of a whole" (71). Here Woolf's satire
of Victorian silliness is at once humorous and pathetic. The make-be-
lieve feminine world of lush novels, oriental romance, teacups, and
phony mysticism is laughable, of course, but it is also the result of a
social system in which the native talents of a Miss Willatt cannot be
channeled effectively because of social strictures and where the need
for reassurance, however muddled, derives from masculine oppression.
Thus, the story cuts several ways at once, recalling wounds Virginia
Woolf had suffered in a Victorian household and as an awkward figure
at dances and parties, exposing the limitations of biography and fiction,
and questioning the social system that creates women as limited as
Miss Linsett and Miss Willatt.

Technically, the story takes Woolf a step closer to the methods she
would soon pioneer. The three-layered story in the guise of a review
essay goes beyond the frame tale method used in "The Journal of Mistress Joan Martyn," and the style has gained in subtlety and sureness.
There is still a touch of Victorian attitudinizing, but now it is tongue-
in-cheek. The self-conscious narrative stance has disappeared, and in
its place is an assured narrator, deftly constructing her complex story
from unlikely materials. The same concerns for women's issues are
expressed, but there is new sophistication in the understanding and

analysis. Beyond this, she is exploring in greater depth the theme that would occupy her for many years—the validity of knowledge as traditionally defined. Clearly Virginia Woolf is continuing to push against the traditional boundaries of story form, stretching them toward the essay. In her next group of stories she would continue this tendency and then suddenly alter course and push the form in the opposite direction—toward the lyric.

Bold Experiments

Rarely does a writer's first published short story mark such an abrupt break with tradition as does "The Mark on the Wall" (1917). From the preceding survey we can see it as an outgrowth of experiments tried earlier and now brought to fruition, but even Woolf's closest friends at the time could not have known this. Nonetheless, it was well received, and the little booklet *Two Stories*, containing this and a tale by Leonard Woolf, sold well as the first production of the Hogarth Press.

The story is cast as a reverie, but not a present one. It is "emotion recollected in tranquility," and curiously the memories themselves are used by the narrator to fix the date, rather than the other way round. As the narrator contemplates the mark on the wall, wondering what it is and using its mysterious presence as a point from which to muse on just about everything, she carries us back to that time in January. Why present it as a recollection, slipping in the first paragraph from past tense to present, as if there were no time barriers? Perhaps because it is a reverie about the unreality of barriers, about the unreality of reality as conventionally defined.

After the introductory paragraph, the story is presented in three sections. In the first, the narrator speculates that the mark may be a nail hole. If so, it may have been left by the people who owned the house previously. Before long, she is musing on the transitoriness of things in our lives and the brevity of life itself. The section ends with reflections on eternity, where one might be "born" and spend fifty years or more as a baby.

The narrator's second guess is that the mark is not a hole but something small and round, a leaf perhaps. Here she focuses on the appeal of reverie, the deliciousness of being alone and letting one's thoughts run where they will. This leads to a passage on the way in which each of us creates himself imaginatively and keeps that creation within bounds, in part by the reactions of others, who are mirrors all around us: "As we face each other in omnibuses and underground railways we are looking into the mirror; that accounts for the vagueness, the gleam of glassiness, in our eyes" (79). This is followed by a clear statement of the central theme: novelists in the future will recognize that reality is in these varied reflections and not in the conventional trappings of "leading articles, cabinet ministers—a whole class of things indeed which as a child one thought the thing itself" (80). Out of this comes a series of reflections on the ridiculous rules based upon such a notion of reality—Victorian ideas about tablecloths and religion.

In the last section, the mark is seen as a projection, a nail perhaps, or a little mound. Around the idea of a mound the narrator creates a humorous portrait of a retired colonel and a country parson unearthing objects from an ancient burial site and speculating endlessly over their interpretation. Then follows an almost angry outburst: what if she verified that it was a nail, would she then have knowledge or just material for further speculation? One could imagine such a lovely world without professors, experts, and the Table of Precedency. Nature herself opposes such speculations, however, and prompts one to verify the facts by direct inspection, since otherwise a clash between the two worlds is inevitable. Such automatic promptings toward verification lead to "our slight contempt for men of action" (82). But the mark, by contrast, is something real—that is, a point from which the imagination may move, as it does now to a reflection on the life of wood and the trees from which wood comes. Furniture is the afterlife of trees. At this point, the meditation ends in "a vast upheaval of matter" (83). Someone else enters the room and identifies the mark as a snail.

If "The Mark on the Wall" were an ordinary story, the preceding paragraphs would be a plot summary. Even in this outline, however, it is clear that Woolf is not writing an essay any more than she is constructing a conventional plot. The movement in the story is imaginative; the links between parts are imagistic and thematic. Although there is a coherent progression of thought, there is no logical order; there is in fact dramatic movement rising to a climax and rapid denouement as the object is finally identified. In the process, the story reenacts the experience it reports, for the prosaic fact of the snail is far less interesting than the speculations it provokes. Imagination is more appealing than reality as commonly defined; fact is as prosaic as the Table of Precedency. The dominant thematic tension in the story is the relation between imagination and fact. Neither is denied, but fact is presented as less appealing than fancy, in part because reliance on it leads to various forms of silliness, like the Table of Precedency, which lists in precise order the relative place of each social title, from monarch to commoner. When social customs and conventions (like traditional fiction) are elevated to the level of reality, we clearly see an element of the ridiculous. Thus, fiction will one day focus on the subjective impressions people have of one another rather than on the so-called substantial world as presented by a writer of realistic fiction. (Here we see the germs of ideas that led eventually to "Modern Fiction.")

An important subtheme in "The Mark on the Wall" is the notion of the afterlife, mentioned in the first and third sections, though in very unorthodox ways. In the first, the narrator imagines being reborn into eternal life (though hardly in the Christian sense these words imply) as a child, where for fifty years or more she can play in a childlike way, "groping at the roots of the grass, or at the toes of the Giants" (78). In the last section, she imparts an eternal life to wood, which begins as a mortal tree but ends as "immortal" furniture. The subtheme is thus a variation on the main one, raising equally interesting questions about reality. Which is the real person, the mortal one in this life or the immortal one in the next—if, of course, that exists? Which is the real tree, the one standing by the stream, shading the cows, or the one turned into furniture and ships? In the former case, all we can know of the afterlife is what we can imagine; in the latter, the facts before us are no less confusing than the leaps of fancy. Small wonder the narrator's head is spinning at the end of the story.

The genius of "The Mark on the Wall" lies not merely in the cleverness of its structure or in the ingenuity of its speculation, but in the drama of the interplay of its images. Speculations that in another treatment could become sterile philosophizing over the nature of reality come alive. Ideas assume almost the stature of characters, their interplay the conflict of plot. Language itself becomes vitalized; truth a matter of a simple phoneme—the difference between nail and snail.

If "The Mark on the Wall" pushes the short story to its essayistic limits, "Kew Gardens" takes the form to the edge of lyric poetry. The inspiration for "Kew Gardens," its lyric mode, and even some of its details may have come from Katherine Mansfield, but the experimentalism of Woolf's early stories and the originality of "The Mark on the Wall" argue against Anthony Alper's suggestion that Mansfield "helped Virginia Woolf to break out of the mould in which she had been working heretofor."[6] There is no denying, however, that these stories mark a genuine departure for Woolf, for perhaps the only factors justifying our calling them stories at all is their overall chronological structure and their use of imaginary incidents and characters. In his carefully reasoned and perceptive essay, "Forms of the Woolfian Short Story," Avrom Fleishman[7] finds both of these stories linear in structure, by which he means that they "start at one place or time or motif or verbal cluster and move through a number of others, arriving at a place, time, motif, or verbal cluster distinct from those with which they begin" (53). Edward L. Bishop (in an essay reprinted here) would identify this linear movement as one toward a "growth of perception" that begins with the oval flower bed and ends in the unity of atmosphere and sound in the story's last paragraph.

These insights into the story's form and unity suggest a third line of inquiry—that "Kew Gardens" is constructed of a series of daring metaphors that call to mind the unifying effect of metaphysical poetry. Just as seventeenth-century poets hoped to reunite a fragmented world by finding similarities in unlike things, so Woolf stretches much of her imagery beyond conventional limits in her effort to unify the story's atmosphere, tone, and effect.

The imagery begins tamely enough with the descriptions of the flowers in the oval bed as having "heart-shaped or tongue-shaped leaves" (84), but soon the metaphors become more daring. The most significant of these at the beginning is the treatment of light as a kind of liquid that stains, falls, expands, settles, and spreads, achieving identification with the water droplets under the flowers before it is once again "flashed into the air above" (84). Light is the transition between the flower bed and the people who move past it like butterflies.

Among these people are the young married couple. He is recalling his first love, a girl named Lily (thus linking her with the flowers in the bed, which from the description could be lilies) whom he remembers chiefly as a shoe with a silver buckle at the toe, while his emotions resembled the dragonfly that hovered round a leaf. His wife recalls an old woman's kiss, "the mother of all my kisses all my life" (85), and describes the present people lying under the trees as ghosts of the past. The effect of these images is to unite light and water, the human world with the natural, the past with the present.

In the following passage, the snail is described as possessing startlingly human characteristics. Unlike the people who stroll aimlessly by, the snail strives toward a goal in a landscape that to its eyes consists of lakes and trees. Meanwhile, two men—one young, materialist, and quiet, the other old, mystical, and animated—stroll past. Their movements also contrast, for "The elder man had a curiously uneven and

shaky method of walking" (86) that resembles the "high-stepping angular green insect" (85) that encountered the snail. The old man, who
may be crazy or merely eccentric, bends his ear to a flower (shaped
like a gramophone trumpet?) and seems to hear a voice. Thus, flowers,
hitherto associated with light and the visible, become part of the au-
dible world. This witty comparison is echoed in the following section
describing two lower-class women, whose "complicated dialogue"
(87), as Woolf ironically calls it, consists mainly of "I says" and "she
says." The thinner woman does most of the talking, to which the stout
one listens at first with a kind of numbed attention. Then she loses
all interest: "She stood there letting the words fall over her, swaying
the top part of her body slowly backwards and forwards, looking at
the flowers" (87). By this description, Woolf indirectly compares the
woman with the flowers, receiving the words as they do light, and
swaying in the wind. Following this incident is another passage describing the snail, imbuing it with human qualities as it considers,
doubts, takes stock, and determines its course.

The last pair to pass the flower bed is a young couple whom Woolf
compares with an emerging flower or butterfly. As Bishop notes, these
lovers, with their hands joined on her parasol as they push it into the
soft soil, become one with the atmosphere of the garden (112–13), but
there is an additional metaphorical unity that they achieve:

> The action and the fact that his hand rested on the top of hers ex-
> pressed their feelings in a strange way, as these short insignificant
> words also expressed something, words with short wings for their
> heavy body of meaning, inadequate to carry them far and thus
> alighting awkwardly upon the very common objects that surrounded
> them and were to their inexperienced touch so massive; but who
> knows . . . what precipices aren't concealed in them, or what slopes
> of ice don't shine in the sun on the other side? (88)

The bee metaphor links the lovers' words to the insect world, itself
part of the flower bed, but beyond that the landscape imagery Woolf
uses to describe the unreliability of language also connects words with
the snail's perception of his tiny world. Looking for something solid to
grasp, the young man fingers a coin and muses on the subjectivity of
reality. Thus, Woolf is not only using language to create a reality but is
commenting on the insubstantiality of both language and reality
themselves.

In the final paragraph, the park dissolves in the heat to a motionless composition, reminding one of Seurat's famous painting. This passage, too, is replete with metaphysical images: a thrush is described as mechanical; butterflies flying one above the other become a "marble column"; roofs resemble umbrellas; colors and shapes become people; voices are like flames from candles.

In the final paradox of the story, silence is revealed to be sound, the steady roar of the city around Kew Gardens, created by the motors and gears of buses, like a "vast nest of Chinese boxes" (89).

"Kew Gardens" is Woolf's first great work of fiction, a prose poem of audacious images and flights of fancy that unite in a grand harmony. It may be true to say that she created nothing of such artistic unity or equal merit until *To the Lighthouse* eight years later.

"The Evening Party" (1918?) remained unpublished until Susan Dick's complete edition of the stories. It represents the first of many stories revolving around the party, a device Woolf frequently used as a microcosm of social types and attitudes. This one has affinities with the drama, as much of it is directly reported dialogue, most of whose speakers are unidentified. The narrator appears as one of these speakers, and the reader is her guest at the party, overhearing conversations and sharing impressions. The tone of the story is breathless and urgent, as if Woolf were whispering excitedly in the reader's ear: "Ah, but let us wait a little!—The moon is up; the sky open; and there, rising in a mound against the sky with trees upon it, is the earth" (90).

Among other things, the story may be an attempt to create a form directly reflecting the nature of the party. Instead of characters, there are a few names and many snatches of unidentified dialogue, just as at a party one seldom sees anything beyond the surface of people and their attitudinizing. The dialogue itself is slick and often trivial, arranged in such a way as to highlight certain attitudes. Thus, the story works by a series of contrasts: nature-artifice, art-life, suffering-frivolity. Woolf is content to identify these conflicts without resolving them or even analyzing their source. If there is an overall theme, it is the nature of literature and criticism, for much of the dialogue contrasts various attitudes toward these—the pedantic professor interested in commas in Shelley's poetry, the socialite too busy to read, the narrator's feeling that there is nothing as perfect in literature as in nature.

Although the method in "The Evening Party" is similar to that of "Kew Gardens," it shows less control. Part of the difficulty is identifying the speakers; the voices are too disembodied and ethereal, and the narrator's own stance is elusive, even flighty. Woolf herself evidently felt the experiment was not worth pursuing through subsequent revisions and hence left the story unfinished.

Late in November 1918, Virginia Woolf wrote to her sister Vanessa Bell that she had just begun a new story about two young men sitting on a beach.[8] The story in progress was "Solid Objects" (1920). The origins of this unusual tale, which resembles an allegory or fable, may be found in Woolf's diary entry for 29 July 1918, in which she describes her visit to the studio of Mark Gertler, an artist she characterized as having more determination than talent. She then goes on to say: "Form obsesses him. . . . Ever since he was a child the solidity & the shapes of objects have tortured him. I advised him, for arts sake, to keep sane; to grasp, & not exaggerate, & put sheets of glass between him & his matter. This, so he said, is now his private wish. But he can think pianola music equal to hand made, since it shows the form, & the touch & the expression are nothing" (*Diary* 1:176).

Professor Watson characterizes "Solid Objects" as an allegory that "diagrams not only a fictional technique, but also the author's odd relations with the things of the world, the interpretive relations that produce stories, but, when they become too rarified and obsessive, also enclose the author with a world of her own devising."[9] The diary entry suggests that the artist in question here is not the author but Gertler, whom Woolf depicts in the story as pursuing his objects obsessively. It is an obsession that begins innocently enough. John (Gertler's fictional name) and his friend Charles are arguing politics as they walk along a beach. They stop beside the shell of a boat for lunch, and while Charles skips flat stones over the water, John burrows into the sand and brings up a lump of green glass. Although John has great promise as a politician, he becomes so absorbed in finding interesting bits of glass, pottery, and iron that he abandons his former ambition and devotes all of his time to finding such objects.

"Solid Objects," then, is a story about an artist's failure to maintain distance and to substitute form for content, serendipity for creation. John could be interpreted as the archetype of artistic purpose and dedication, but Woolf makes it clear that he carries his passion beyond measure. His delight in the lump of green glass is first depicted as childlike, and the objects for a time serve as practical paperweights. In the end, however, John's obsession cuts him off from human society;

he has nothing to say to others. When Charles visits for a last time, he accuses John of having given up. John disagrees, but then Charles of course means politics, while John thinks he is referring to his collection. Failure to communicate is a recurring theme in Woolf's writing,[10] and here she seems to be concerned with the artist's exclusive obsession with form. In this respect, "Solid Objects" resembles Kafka's "Hunger Artist," only in Woolf's story it is not the public that fails to appreciate the artist's purity, but the artist's singlemindedness that cuts him off from the public.

"Sympathy" (1919) resembles "The Mark on the Wall," only in the later story the subject is death, and the purpose of the meditation is to understand death and its effects on the living. The writer's first reaction to reading the obituary of her friend Humphry Hammond is pain mixed with regret that she did not get to know Humphry better, did not take the time to draw him out and understand him the last time he and his wife, Celia, visited. The writer then tries to imagine Celia at the unknowable moment as she transforms herself from wife to widow. It is not Celia's grief that she dwells upon, but her knowledge and security, by which she presumably means the certainty that comes with knowing one cannot again be hurt and surprised by death. This the narrator envies. Envy gives way to compassion, however, as she imagines Celia bravely coping with her loss; she pictures herself on a country walk with Celia, which ends in the discovery of a thrush's nest and five eggs. The eggs suggest birth, the boundary between being and nonbeing at the beginning of life; death is analogous, another boundary we must cross to see the pattern in our lives and those of our friends. The death of others, then, forces her to confront the brevity of life and to admit that she has been callous toward death's latest victim. At this point the reverie is interrupted by the arrival of an invitation from the Hammonds to dine. Humphry is not dead: "O why did you deceive me?" (105) is the story's last line.

It is hard to know what to make of this complex and beautifully written piece, which resembles an essay and a lyric poem at the same time. A clue may perhaps be found in a brief diary entry made near the time this story was written. After hearing of the death of Florence Darwin, Woolf asks herself, "If I now heard that this letter . . . was untrue, I should try to see her again. But what is it that prevents one from ever seeing people, when years have passed, & there have been deaths & births & marriages?" (*Diary* 2:25). The story does not so much answer this question as explore the possibilities of feeling aroused by death and the irritation one would feel if she were to mourn and then learn that the mourning was unnecessary. The angry outburst at the story's end is directed at a generalized "you," which could be interpreted as referring to Humphry, the newspaper, or her own jumping to conclusions. Death has aroused a wide range of emotions, from envy to sympathy, regret to anger; its "immense power" (104) lies in the shape it gives to fleeting life.

"An Unwritten Novel" (1920) has often been compared to "The Mark on the Wall," "The Shooting Party" (1938), and "The Lady in the Looking-Glass" (1929) for its reverie and imaginative reflection on an external object. In these stories, however, the object is another human being rather than a mark, and because of that there can be no simple verification of the hypotheses as there was in the first of these. Moreover, "An Unwritten Novel" occurred at a crucial time in Woolf's development, when she had outgrown the conventional trappings of fiction as evidenced by *Night and Day* (1919) and was moving in the direction that would culminate in *Jacob's Room* (1922). Woolf's biographer Lyndall Gordon sees in "An Unwritten Novel" a foretaste of "the comic drama of a writer in pursuit of a subject" evident in *Jacob's Room*.[11] Something of Woolf's experimental mood and direction may be seen in a diary entry written shortly after this story was published and the novel was in progress:

> Well, but I assure you, when Virginia's old, no one will be talking of Romer Wilson. What a book! What a perfect example of the faux bon: every attitude, scene & word, I should say matched in the old word shop of the minor poets: never a single thing seen for herself, or dared; & yet by taking all the scenery & supplying the appropriate words she has Squire, Lynd, & Turner {book reviewers} by the heel: another proof that what people dread is being made to feel anything: a certain kind of rhapsody makes them feel wild & adventurous; & they then make out that this is passion and poetry—so thankful to be let off the genuine thing. (*Diary* 2:117)

The attitude expressed here is identical to that of "Modern Fiction." Woolf is striving toward something beyond the trappings of realistic fiction, something that will take the reader into consciousness and feeling. As in "The Mark on the Wall," the feelings explored in "An Unwritten Novel" are largely those of the narrator, even though on the surface the story appears to be about the person seated opposite her in a railway carriage, an elderly woman whom she calls Minnie Marsh. Stephen D. Fox was the first to point out that the details included about Minnie Marsh are almost entirely of the narrator's imagining and that therefore the character revealed is that of the fanciful writer. The theme of the story, therefore, is not just "the elusiveness of external reality" but "the essence of the narrator's personality" as revealed "by her secret responses."[12] This parallels a passage in "The Mark on the Wall" asserting that the people we face in trains and buses are reflections of ourselves.

Fox's analysis is certainly correct, but the nature of Woolf's insight into the narrator can be pushed further than the irony at the end of the story where the narrator's conclusions about Minnie Marsh's unhappy life are dashed by the arrival of her affectionate son. The first clue is the title itself, an allusion perhaps to the cliché that every person's life is worthy of a novel or an indication that the narrator is herself a novelist. The exact interpretation is unimportant, since either leads to the same place—that the narrator is attempting to assemble a kind of novel from the scanty clues available. Judging from the world-weary eyes of all the passengers in the compartment and in particular from Minnie Marsh's expression, the narrator concludes that life is a pretty dreary business and that humans do their best to conceal this knowledge from one another. Proof of this assumption, as it were, is found in the incessant reporting of bad news as carried in the *Times*, behind which the narrator hides. As the train progresses, other people in the compartment leave, until Minnie Marsh and the narrator are left alone. At this point, they exchange a few words, mostly platitudes, but Minnie Marsh complains aloud of her sister-in-law in a voice "like lemon on cold steel" (107). On the basis of this hint the narrator begins her first round of reveries concerning Minnie Marsh's life. At this point she feels closest to her subject, repeating Minnie's phrase about sisters-in-law, rubbing an indelible spot on the window just as Minnie does, and even sharing an itch between the shoulder blades. Feeling this closely identified with her subject, she believes she has "deciphered her secret" (108).

But her deciphering takes the form of clichés from popular fiction. The sister-in-law is dubbed Hilda and becomes domineering and condescending to the inept and spinsterish Minnie. Minnie's God is imagined in the crudest terms, as President Kruger of Germany, and her itch derives from a Lady Macbeth sense of guilt, brought on by a dereliction of duty that resulted in the scalding death of a child. Clearly, this novelist's fancy runs to lurid melodrama and stereotyping, as in the next scene, where we see Minnie pinching her pennies at a seaside resort, living a life of excessive caution and prissiness. In a lyrical interlude, the author questions the accuracy of her musings, but when Minnie takes a hard-boiled egg from her handbag and begins shelling it, the novelist interprets this as confirmation of her method and proceeds with more set pieces, these surrounding Minnie's relationship with a married button salesman named "Muggeridge." The passage is drenched in social clichés, from his middle-class eating habits to his table among the aspidistras. All of these details, we are assured, are not the narrator's fault but life's. The narrator would like to color her tale with rhododendrons and someone named Rose, but verisimilitude prevents her. And so we watch Minnie, like a figure in a bad play, bemoan her fate in a lonely bedroom with claret-colored curtains. The only consolations the novelist can offer poor Minnie are a faithful dog and clean underlinen (complete with a reference to the old maid's admonition that one should always wear clean underwear in case of accident or emergency when doctors and nurses would see). All this reaches its climax just as the train pulls into the station.

As Minnie leaves the train, she is met by her son, not her censorious sister-in-law, and the narrator is amazed to see them go off happily together. This reverses everything the would-be novelist has invented and forces her to change her mind: the story suddenly ceases to be a tragic study of guilt and spinsterhood and becomes cheerful. The author sheds her previous pessimism and declares, "it's you, unknown figures, you I adore; if I open my arms, it's you I embrace, you I draw to me—adorable world" (115). This is simply jumping from one extreme to the other, missing the truth about Minnie Marsh as surely as the earlier story. For we know from Minnie's own words that she has trouble with her sister-in-law; she is irritated about something. Thus to suddenly give the story a "happy ending" is as clichéd as to presume from external signals that Minnie's life is tragic. This is a novelist who imagines in clichés and writes in formulas. The story, therefore, is not simply about the limits of the imagination but also about the limits of the kind of stuff that normally passes for fiction. Not just the form but the content also needs reform, and this is what Virginia Woolf strived for in her own writing.

"A Haunted House" (1921) has affinities to "Sympathy" in dealing with unseen webs of human relations and to "Kew Gardens" in evoking atmosphere and connecting people to a specific place. It also reverses the usual clichés about the spirit world by presenting a pair of benign and friendly ghosts who make their presence felt by hunting about the house for a lost something, thereby disturbing the present owners and their possessions. As in "The Mark on the Wall," we are not certain until the end what the "it" is that the ghostly couple seeks throughout the house and garden; indeed, the writer is not sure until the last line. But as "it" hovers in suspense, the feeling grows that whatever it is, it is something quiet and tender, a "buried treasure" of more than material value. This is evident in the story's quiet tone and in the writer's gentle assurances that the ghosts' effects are subtle and unthreatening. The pigeons that bubble outside the windows, the green leaves, and the hum of the threshing machine in the distance are among the many details that reassure both narrator and reader.

All we learn of the ghosts apart from their friendly intent is that they inhabited the house long ago. When the woman died, her husband left on far-flung journeys, finally returning as a ghost to find the house safe. They have become the pulse beat of the home, its guarantee of warmth and safety. At the conclusion, the narrator awakens with the spirit couple apparently watching over her sleep and realizes that their treasure is "The light in the heart" (117). The story is thus gentle and reassuring, evoking a sense of mystery and wonder, not terror, and suggesting the enduring power of love and the peacefulness of death.

"Monday or Tuesday," the title story of the slender volume Virginia Woolf published in 1921, "Blue and Green" (1921), and "In the Orchard" (1923) are meditative sketches with even less narrative than "Kew Gardens." These are the most poetic of Woolf's prose writings, making no pretense at telling a story or even making a point, at least in the conventional senses. They are perhaps best regarded as experiments in the lyric possibilities of prose. Virginia's letters of this period shed no light on her intent in these stories, but in the diary entries from 6 March 1921 through 17 February 1922 we get occasional glimpses into her hopes for them. Shortly before the book was published, she tried to exorcise the demon of fear of bad reviews by anticipating what would be said of her little book. She says in part, "Then, in the Westminster, Pall Mall, other serious evening papers I shall be treated very shortly, with sarcasm. The general line will be that I am becoming too much in love with the sound of my own voice: not much in what I write: indecently [?] affected; a disagreeable woman" (*Diary* 2:98). A month later, just as the book was being released, she was upset by a brief notice in the *Times*: "they don't see that I'm after something interesting" (*Diary* 2:106). Her depression gave way to happiness, however, as good reviews began to appear, and her friends added their praises. Her diary records particularly the praise of Roger Fry, who thought her "on the track of real discoveries" (*Diary* 2:109), and T. S. Eliot, who liked "String Quartet" and found "Haunted House" "extremely interesting" (*Diary* 2:125). A year later, when a tepid review of the American edition of her work appeared in the *Dial* (New York), she assumed a defensive posture by claiming that she would write as she liked and let the critics do the same (*Diary* 2:166).

Perhaps the most interesting feature of these diary entries is their sensitivity to the opinions of others, particularly reviewers and the public as reflected in sales. We are accustomed to thinking of Virginia Woolf in particular and of Bloomsbury in general as aloof from public opinion, but Woolf was very sensitive, and her mood fluctuated with the tenor of her reviews. The few hints we gather about her intent in these stories are sufficient only to verify that she was consciously experimenting, looking for a voice and style of her own, using her prose to push toward something new and unexpected. Just what she was searching for in these vignettes can be ascertained only indirectly through the stories themselves.

"Monday or Tuesday" will strike some readers as delightfully suggestive and others as perversely obscure. Its events, if we can call them that, seem ordered in time beginning with the outward flight of a heron and ending with its return. Between these two relatively distinct brackets—the most conventional and grammatical passages in the sketch—occur the random events of a typical day—the movement of buses, the tolling of a clock, the drinking of tea, the lighting of hearth fires. Entangled with these are long, dangling participial phrases and recurrent, fragmentary references to truth. The intent of these devices may be to contrast the relatively orderly world of nature, as represented by the heron and the sky, with the disorderly and often trivial human world, absorbed in its daily cares and heedless of truth. The structural and grammatical ambiguities are complicated by wordplay. "Desiring truth," for instance, could modify something or someone unspecified who desires truth or could be taken to mean that truth desires something. "Down that falls" could refer to the setting of the sun or to the sun's rays as they move down a mountain slope. "Radiating to a point" on one level makes no sense, since things radiate from rather than to a point, or it could modify the firelight mentioned later in the sentence.

Whether we label such an experiment as successful or unsuccessful will depend largely on how we define sucess. If we agree with scientists who say that even a null result makes a worthwhile experiment, then we are likely to see this and other sketches of the type as worthy of attempt, but of limited practical application. Incidentally, the use of parentheses in this piece resembles the way e. e. cummings used them in his poetry. In both Virginia Woolf's story and cummings's poetry, parentheses suggest simultaneous action rather than grammatical subordination. Both are pushing against the boundaries of written language toward something like painting or music.

"Blue and Green" treats green light as a liquid, just as was done in the opening lines of "Kew Gardens." Its two paragraphs comprise an elaborate conceit on this resemblance, first treating a pool of green light that collects on a white marble tabletop as an oasis around which cluster other green things, until the green of day is swept away by the blue of night. Blue creates its own ocean in which a whale cavorts, beaches itself, and dies. The concluding sentence describes the cold interior of a cathedral, with only a faint blue emanating from statues of the Virgin.

The experiment here seems to be with the suggestive power of color and with "metaphysical" imagery. The chief point in these paragraphs is the play of imagination on the phenomenon of light; in this sense there is a childlike quality in the exuberance of the writer's fancy. The last sentence describing the cathedral suggests a contrast between the cycles of nature and the artificiality of human institutions, although this may attribute too much philosophy to what may be simply a tonal variation.

"In the Orchard" is considerably longer than either of these two sketches and is dated a year or so later (Dick, 295). It resembles them closely enough, however, to justify our discussing it here. The sketch is divided into three parts, each of which describes the same scene—Miranda asleep beneath the apple trees. The first begins with Miranda and ascends through layers of sound—the voices of school children, the drunken cry of a cattle drover, the music of the church organ, the prayers of the rector, and finally the squeak of the weathervane on the church tower, which awakens Amanda in time for tea. The second section entertains the possibility that Miranda is not asleep but thinking and relates her thoughts to the levels of sound described in the first part. Her thoughts vary from the mundane to the fanciful and end, as before, with her realizing that it is time for tea. The third section offers a different point of view entirely, confining itself to the orchard and the land surrounding it. Like the other two it begins with Miranda on the ground and ends with her jumping up to go to tea.

Taken together, these three views provide a composite sketch of the scene. The first two may be seen as vertical, the first ascending from Miranda through the various layers of sight and sound, the second descending into Miranda's consciousness through separate levels of thought and imagination. The final view is a lateral one, moving no higher than the branches of the apple trees and concentrating on sights and events within the orchard itself and the space just beyond it. The overall effect is thus not unlike that of a draftsman's orthographic projection—three views that, taken together, give a full rendering of a three dimensional object on a two dimensional surface.

Another comparison might be found in the school of imagist poets, writing at about the same time as Woolf was composing these sketches. One finds in both an exactness of language, a freedom in choice of subject, a concentration of thought, and an attempt to render a concrete object in words. Such a comparison should not be pushed too far, particularly in light of Woolf's own reluctance to explain her intentions; but the similarities are striking. Moreover, both these sketches and imagist poetry place great demands on the reader's ingenuity, patience, and tolerance for novelty. Certainly Virginia Woolf is capitalizing on the freedom provided her by the Hogarth Press to explore the limits of prose in ways commercial publishers would probably not have allowed her to do.

In sharp contrast to the art-for-art's sake nature of these sketches are two stories of overt social criticism. The first and most obviously political is "A Society" (1921). This story derives from Virginia Woolf's part in the famous *Dreadnought* hoax. Interested readers should consult Quentin Bell's hilarious account of the incident[13]; suffice it here to say that Woolf joined five male friends disguised as Abyssinian dignitaries, and the entourage was given an official guided tour by the Royal Navy of the new and secret battleship *Dreadnought*. The resulting furor in newsprint and in Parliament convinced Woolf, if she needed further convincing, that the male world of honor and politics was childish and absurd. It is also likely, as Susan Dick points out, that the story is a reaction to essays by Arnold Bennett and Desmond MacCarthy on the innate inferiority of women's intelligence.[14] "A Society" is a sprightly satire on this childish male world and on men's condescending attitudes toward women.

Six young women are discussing men one day when they decide to judge what centuries of male domination have produced. They conclude that the object of life is to "produce good people and good books" (120), and each is given an area of life to investigate. Later, they share their results: Rose gives a report on honor as practiced in the Royal Navy (based, of course, on the Navy's reactions to the *Dreadnought* affair); Fanny gives an account of judges in law courts; Helen analyzes pictures in the Royal Academy; Castalia finds the scholars of Oxford and Cambridge trivial and dull. When Castalia becomes pregnant, despite the friends' collective vow of chastity, she is not ostracized, but her condition does prompt the women to conclude that until men improve, artificial insemination might be preferable to marriage.

World War I intervenes and curtails the friends' investigations; when it is almost over, Castalia and Cassandra (the narrator) peruse the group's minutes and conclude that their greatest mistake was to believe in man's intellect. They further suggest that unless they can figure out a way to have men bear children, the world will destroy itself. When the peace treaty is signed, they turn over the Society to Castalia's daughter, and she weeps.

What saves "A Society" from being just a political tract is its puckish good humor and pell-mell pace. On the surface it is a farce, an intellectual romp through the pomposities and absurdities of men and their institutions. The women are portrayed at first as naive; as their disenchantment with men grows and their investigations proceed, the story acquires shape and suspense. By having the women investigate and draw conclusions about the accomplishments of men, Woolf gives her characters an air of astonished innocence. There is little suggestion that women are superior to men; what they lament as much as anything is an education that makes them able for the first time to question their position and the value of men's work without empowering them to make useful contributions or reforms. They might, they surmise, be better off ignorant and bearing children, like their mothers. Perhaps it would be best to interpret "A Society" as a tale of lost innocence as much as a satire on men or as a volley in the battle between the sexes. What Castalia's daughter weeps over is not her sex but the knowledge that she must carry on the work of a society that will make her as dissatisfied as her mother. Thus the humor of the story cuts two ways: it not only lampoons outrageous male behavior but also suggests the difficulty women face in dealing with their newfound insights. "A Society" may not be great fiction, but it shows a side of Virginia Woolf that is seldom discussed—her capacity for fun and her sense of the absurd.

"A Woman's College from Outside" was not published until 1926, but according to Susan Dick was likely written in 1920 (294–95). In theme and method, too, it belongs with the group of stories we have been discussing rather than with the later period. Like many of the stories already discussed, this one is not so much a narrative as an atmospheric piece. It describes Newnham College late at night. Most of the students are sleep, but Angela is awake, working hard on economics, mindful of her parents' sacrifice in sending her to university. In another room, a group of young women plays cards, enjoying the freedom of the late night—"this irresponsible laughter: this laughter of mind and body floating away rules, hours, discipline" (141). Part of the story's poignance comes from the contrast between these girls' irresponsible ease and Angela's industry, but the overall tone is poetic, almost rhapsodic. Woolf captures brilliantly, without herself ever having attended university, the delicious freedom and anticipation of student life, its reaching toward the promising future.

Angela feels these emotions, and the bright world beneath the moon reflects her mood: it too seems new, fresh, and suspended in anticipation. If the story has a message, it is one of hope for a new generation of young women—educated and hence able to play some part in the world beyond that traditionally assigned them. Knowing that this promise was a long way from being fulfilled in Virginia Woolf's lifetime does not make the story sentimental, for what she has captured here is more than the mood of a woman's college; it is the aspirations of youth, seasoned with just enough spice of social reality to prevent it from cloying sweetness. It is a delicious fragment, showing yet another aspect of Virginia Woolf's ability to create memorable experiences from ordinary materials.

"The String Quartet" (1921) bears comparison with several stories discussed above, especially "The Evening Party." Both concern social events, both contrast the triviality of everyday life with the beauty and permanence of art, and both are narrated by an anonymous voice who speaks in the first person plural. As in the earlier story, it is difficult to tell whom the narrator is addressing—the reader, an unnamed companion, or the narrator herself. Indeed, one of the central interpretive problems of this and other of Virginia Woolf's stories is this issue of authorial voice—a problem similar to that encountered in reading her novels. It is complicated in this story by the fact that much of it appears to be interior monologue in reaction to the music played by the string quartet, although even here it is not always possible to tell when music is playing and when it is not. The overall effect is to merge and confuse the interior and exterior worlds into an exploration of various levels of consciousness that blend into one another.

As already noted, one of the story's themes is the triviality of everyday life. Snatches of overheard conversation, dialogues between the narrator and unnamed others, and descriptions of the audience's concerns, including those of the narrator, make this point abundantly clear. In contrast is the music of the string quartet, whose first selection is a piece by Mozart to which the narrator responds with a romantic, indeed rhapsodic, description of the Rhone River teeming with fish, and of fat, obscene fishwives. This reverie is interrupted by what appears to be a number of remarks by the narrator to someone else—perhaps the same person addressed in the beginning of the story, perhaps not. In any event, the music has awakened contradictory emotions—hope, despair, joy, and a desire for obscene stories. The music then resumes, perhaps with a slow movement from the same piece, for again the dominant images are of water and a river. More dialogue and a description of blind Mrs. Munro seem to indicate an intermission. When the music resumes, it brings to mind snatches from a romantic novel or opera involving a lady in distress and a sword fight. Out of this comes a vision of an ancient or perhaps Middle Eastern city, a sort of palace of art that seems a secure respite from ordinary confusion: "Firm establishment. Fast foundations. March of myriads. Confusion and chaos trod to earth. But this city to which we travel has neither stone nor marble; hangs enduring; stands unshakable; nor does a face, nor does a flag greet or welcome. Leave then to perish your hope; droop in the desert my joy; naked advance. Bare are the pillars; auspicious to none; casting no shade; resplendent; severe" (135). The contrary emotions aroused by the music are not so much resolved as unified, as in a work of art. The narrator desires at this point only to leave, reentering the world of everyday trivia.

"The String Quartet" is not a story "about" anything, although it does contain a number of ideas. Instead, it re-creates experience as directly as possible through the medium of words. Moreover, although Woolf's diary (*Diary* 2:24) records an excursion to a concert for the express purpose of taking notes for a story, presumably this one, it is not external reality that the story seeks to re-create so much as the contrast or interplay between the objective and subjective. If this interplay is viewed as a contest, then as usual the subjective and interior triumphs over the objective and exterior, even though it appears to do so more as a relief from the ordinary than as an absolute preference for the spiritual.

Exploring Character

There is no great change in Virginia Woolf's short fiction during the "middle period" as defined here. The years 1923–29 still find her experimenting with style and form, but the experiments are different from those discussed above. She had explored what could be accomplished by setting, atmosphere, and structure, and she sets out to seek new opportunities, particularly in character development. In her important essay "Mr. Bennett and Mrs. Brown" (1924) she had reacted to Arnold Bennett's assertion that in fiction character is the most important element by analyzing shrewdly the techniques of Bennett, Wells, and Galsworthy, finding them all wanting by Bennett's criterion—or at least as it applied to Georgian, as opposed to Edwardian, ideas of what constitutes character. As in "Modern Fiction," she insists that what occurs inside the character's mind is more important than the superficial facts of income, class, or dress. Addressing her audience directly, she says near the end of her lecture: "You have gone to bed at night bewildered by the complexity of your feelings. In one day thousands of ideas have coursed through your brains; thousands of emotions have met, collided, and disappeared in astonishing disorder. Nevertheless, you allow the writers to palm off upon you a version of all this, an image of Mrs. Brown, which has no likeness to that surprising apparition whatsoever."[15]

The stories of Woolf's middle period work out in more detail than the earlier ones the implications of this insight. Many focus on character from the inside; they are frequently interior monologues interrupted by exterior events or moments of description. The clash between the character's thoughts and feelings with events in the environment often produces conflict and tension, making them seem more dramatic and thus more recognizable as stories than many of the earlier experiments. Nevertheless, many of the same forces are at work, most notably extreme compression of thought and language. Again, a quotation from the essay links practice with theory: "The writer's task is to take one thing and let it stand for twenty: a task of danger and difficulty; but only so is the reader relieved of the swarm and confusion of life and branded effectively with the particular aspect which the writer wishes him to see" (*Essays* 2:135). The style, in response to the change of emphasis, is less descriptive and lyrical but no less complex and taut. Long, complicated, apparently loose but really tightly knit sentences attempt to express the pressure of conflicting thoughts and emotions. Whereas earlier stories pushed the limits of the genre, these struggle against the confines of the English sentence, many of which are periodic in construction, suspending some crucial element until the end. What had been an observable tendency in the earlier stories becomes an habitual device in this period.

It is difficult to say whether these stories represent an "advance" over the earlier ones, but they certainly represent a change in that several center on a single party given by Mrs. Dalloway. Since these have been conveniently collected by Stella McNichol and since they have a unity of their own, it will be most advantageous to discuss them together in the order in which (so far as can be determined) they were written.

"Mrs. Dalloway in Bond Street" (1923) was perhaps first conceived as the opening chapter of the novel *Mrs. Dalloway* (1925).[16] Like a number of other stories, this one moves on two levels: the narrative plane of exterior action and a parallel one of Mrs. Dalloway's thoughts. On the first level, we follow Mrs. Dalloway as she walks up Bond Street, meets an old acquaintance, enters a shop, peruses several pairs of gloves, and finally is startled by a backfiring automobile. These actions are not merely incidental, since many of her thoughts during this time are triggered by exterior events, but the real action of the story is the interior monologue. According to Judith Saunders, the central and controlling allusion of her thoughts is a passage from Shelley's elegiac poem, "Adonais." Analyzing the train of Clarissa Dalloway's thoughts and focusing particularly on the repetitions of the line "From the contagion of the world's slow stain," Saunders concludes that Mrs. Dalloway associates the stain with menstruation and hence with female weakness. She summarizes, "Superficial attempts at brisk cheerfulness notwithstanding, the predominant mood of 'Mrs. Dalloway in Bond Street' is one of futility and resignation. Regarding herself as soiled, weak and unfit, Clarissa concludes that 'one doesn't live for oneself' {152}, that woman is doomed to the role of spectator in all the grandest of life's experiences. Despite its clear relationship to *Mrs. Dalloway*, the 'Bond Street' story denies the connections between death and life which triumph in the novel. Instead Clarissa looks to death to free her from the bodily and spiritual degradation of being female."[17]

Insightful as Professor Saunders's reading is, one need not accept its gloomy conclusions about the story. Admittedly, from its opening observation about the chiming of Big Ben and indeed about the famous clock's internal decay, the story is about the passing of time and hence about advancing age and even death. At the same time, it is useful to recall that Shelley's poem is about the premature death of a great poet, Keats, and that it is not death itself but the world that "stains." To Clarissa, the "hour was fresh as if issued to children on a beach" (146), and she is observed by Scope Purvis, C. B., as a "charming woman, poised, eager, strangely white-haired for her pink cheeks" (146). What Mr. Purvis sees, the author confirms, describing her thus: "Pride held her erect, inheriting, handing on, acquainted with discipline and with suffering" (146).

No sooner has the point about suffering been made than Mrs. Dalloway meets her old friend Hugh Whitbread, who has brought his wife to visit a Harley Street physician. From Whitbread's manner, Clarissa guesses "female troubles," probably menopause, as his wife's problem, prompting her to think of the physical disadvantages of being female and the social liabilities that ensue from these. Rather than accept this judgment, however, as Professor Saunders implies, Mrs. Dalloway rejects it: "For there is this extraordinarily deep instinct, something inside one; you can't get over it; it's no use trying; and men like Hugh respect it without our saying it, which is what one loves, thought Clarissa, in dear old Hugh" (147). It is this last phrase "dear old Hugh" that makes the difference. By its condescending tone, Mrs. Dalloway rejects the notion that women are biologically prevented from doing things that men traditionally do. Much of the rest of the story seems to reinforce this rejection.

In this next section, Mrs. Dalloway considers Queen Victoria and the present queen, possessed of "character" and able to perform useful work. A chance association reminds her of remarks made last night about Jack Stewart, who died an untimely death. This, in turn, brings to mind Shelley's line, followed by a welter of associations, internal and external, ending in the thought that the modern poets have produced no memorable work on death. The contrast between past and present is reinforced by the sight of a young woman, overly made up and asleep in a car, evidently exhausted after a night of dancing. Clarissa disapproves of the frivolity and the makeup. Turning into Bond Street, she sees Lady Bexborough waiting in a carriage. Lady Bexborough, we later learn, is a tragic figure who lost her favorite son in the war, yet bravely carried on opening a bazaar even while the telegram was still in her hand. This leads Clarissa to reflect that if her husband died, she too would carry on "For the sake of others" (152). Between these thoughts about Lady Bexborough, Mrs. Dalloway has entered the shop and begun to look at gloves. She recalls her uncle's maxim that a lady is known by her gloves and shoes and hopes that no dowdy women come to her party, incidentally asking herself, "Would one have liked Keats if he had worn red socks?" (151). Trying on a pair of gloves, she considers the shop girl sympathetically, not wanting to be too troublesome, lest this be the one day of the month when to stand would be painful for her. A moment later, she again recalls Shelley's line, this time in connection with age spots on her arm—a reminder of her own mortality. Then another customer enters the shop, a woman Clarissa thinks she knows, and as she waits, a line from *Cymbeline* repeats itself in her head: "Fear no more the heat of the sun." By this time, Mrs. Dalloway is growing impatient with the slow-moving shop girl, but suddenly all thoughts are ended by an explosion in the street and her sudden recognition of the other woman. The passage is instructive: "There was a violent explosion in the street outside. The shopwomen cowered behind the counters. But Clarissa, sitting very upright, smiled at the other lady. 'Miss Anstruther!' she exclaimed" (153).

As already noted, one of the recurring themes of this story is the passage of time and the eventuality of death, but this is balanced by instances of courage in the face of these enemies. Pride and discipline, the feminine virtues alluded to repeatedly throughout the story, are emphasized at its end by the unflappability of Mrs. Dalloway and Miss Anstruther. To be sure, there is an element of class snobbery in Mrs. Dalloway's attitude: she does not like dowdy women, and she gives more weight to the courage of Lady Bexborough than to that of the shop girl. Men, indeed, may undervalue women, bar them from Parliament, and emphasize the trivialities of gloves and shoes, but Mrs. Dalloway, while recognizing the ravages of time, does not bow before age, death, or disappointment. Moreover, the sons who are dying to make this life possible are not depicted as more heroic than the women who mourn their loss. In short, it is possible to read this story as consistent with Virginia Woolf's other stories about <u>feminine ability</u>—as an affirmation of the strength of the female character in spite of the social disadvantages from which women suffer.

"The New Dress" (1925; publ. 1927) is perhaps the most directly autobiographical of the party stories. Its central character, Mabel Waring, comes to Mrs. Dalloway's party wearing a new dress that had seemed appropriate enough in the dressmaker's shop but now strikes her as ludicrously unsuitable. Most of the story re-creates her thoughts about the dress, all of which are negative and full of self-flaggelation and recrimination. Abruptly, she leaves the party early, hypocritically thanking her hostess and saying that she has enjoyed herself. No episode in Virginia Woolf's life closely parallels these events, but as we saw in the discussion of "Phyllis and Rosamond," she often felt self-conscious and out of place at parties. Numerous entries in her letters and diaries complain about the pain of attending social gatherings and particularly about the problem of finding suitable clothes. The most relevant to this story is recorded for 30 June 1926, very close to the time Virginia Woolf was working on "The New Dress":

> This is the last day of June & finds me in black despair because Clive {Bell} laughed at my new hat. . . . Well, it was after they {the guests} had come & we were all sitting round talking that Clive suddenly said, or bawled rather, what an astonishing hat you're wearing! Then he asked where I got it. I pretended a mystery, tried to change the talk, was not allowed, & they pulled me down between them, like a hare; I never felt more humiliated. Clive said did Mary choose it? No. Todd {Miss Todd, editor of *Vogue*} said Vita {Sackville-West}. And the dress? Todd of course: after that I was forced to go on as if nothing terrible had happened; but it was very forced & queer & humiliating. So I talked and laughed too much. Duncan {Grant} prim and acid as ever told me it was utterly impossible to do anything with a hat like that. (*Diary* 3:90–91)

The individual reference is less important than the overall insecurity Virginia Woolf felt for much of her life about her appearance and her performance at parties.[18] Much of this was transferred to her short fiction, particularly in the person of Mabel Waring.

The striking difference between the incident related in Virginia Woolf's diary and the situation in "The New Dress" is that all of the negative feelings come from Mabel Waring herself. No one in the story comments adversely on her appearance; in fact, several people notice her new dress and praise it. Mabel's innate insecurity is the source of her misery: she regards all compliments as lies and interprets all remarks and gestures as criticism. Her feelings of self-loathing (and that is what they amount to) spring in part from her lower middle-class origins where, at least in her view, nothing was every wholly successful or prosperous—a cheese-paring, penny-pinching, watery-blooded family. Thus, she feels like a fly trapped in a saucer of milk, while the others are elegant and beautiful butterflies or dragonflies. Her painful feelings at the party are intensified by memories of happiness at the dressmaker's, where she felt a sudden rush of love and pity for the toiling Miss Milan. Here, not only the party itself but also her feelings of shame at caring so much for the opinion of others have reduced her to "a feeble, vacillating creature" (168). In contrast to her social insecurity are the feelings she gets by thinking how heroic she might have been as the wife of an empire builder or by recalling delicious moments of her private and domestic life. But these are overwhelmed by waves of anxiety: "She had always been a fretful, weak, unsatisfactory mother, a wobbly wife, lolling about in a kind of twilight existence with nothing very clear or very bold or more one thing than another" (170). Her only solace is a moment of romantic reverie in which she imagines herself magically transformed by a book or person into someone noble and admirable. At this idea, she leaves the party.

If it is safe to say that Virginia Woolf on occasion shared Mabel Waring's feelings of inferiority, it is also true to say that in this story she holds these feelings up to the light of reason and finds them understandable but irrational. Mabel Waring is not despised by the others at the party; in fact, from another story, "A Simple Melody," we have direct evidence to the contrary (195–96). Her humiliation is self-inflicted. By the same token, the story implicitly criticizes the social system for creating conditions in which a woman's worth can be assessed by her clothes. There is no chance at the party, and by extension in society, for Mabel Waring to pursue her ambitions or express her feelings. Mabel judges herself and the other women at the party in large measure by external appearance; enviously she regards the fashionable elegance of Rose Shaw.

The other side of the female dilemma, a life of domestic work, is represented by Mrs. Holman, who takes no thought for clothes, concentrating all of her energies on the family. Mrs. Waring despises her and resents being asked questions about holidays and children. She sees their reflections in a convex mirror that reduces them to the size of one yellow and one black button. The mirror, in Mabel Waring's mind, reflects their status as women. "The New Dress," therefore, is like "Phyllis and Rosamond," a story about the limits women face and the artificiality of these boundaries. It is a recurring theme in these party stories.

"Happiness" (1925) contrasts sharply with "The New Dress" in focusing on Stuart Elton, a theatrical man completely satisfied with himself and his lot in life. This indefinable feeling of his, which he does not call happiness, is perhaps best understood as wholeness—"to be at one" (172). This feeling is threatened by the attentions of Mrs. Sutton, an actress whose career is stalled. Their conversation lasts only a few moments, but in this brief, telescoped time Elton's thoughts and responses to Mrs. Sutton's comments reveal him to be a complex, elusive character. His attitude toward her is polite but evasive; he has what she wants—not simply success in the theater—but self-assurance and confidence. By his gesture of flicking a thread from his trousers he hopes to deflect her advances, like a man in a sled fleeing wolves who distracts them by tossing bits of biscuit for them to fight over. He wants to evade her not because he resents her wanting his professional support but because he resists all threats to his independence. His happiness stems not from the usual attributes of love or health but from a "mystic state" that "freed him from all dependence upon anyone upon anything" (174).

The difficulty is to detect the author's attitude toward Stuart Elton. Does she regard him as a selfish, self-congratulating prig, or does she envy or even approve of his self-contained wholeness? There are few clues in the story itself, apart from the disappointment—even humiliation—Mrs. Sutton feels at being rejected by him. And rejected she is, for in the middle of their talk he abruptly leaves to reassure himself that his independence is still intact. If this signal is the vital clue, and perhaps it is, then Stuart Elton is one of several men in this series of stories who offend by having the luxury of such confidence, such indifference to others. Elton is less aggressive and outwardly obnoxious toward others than males we will later meet, but he shares with them the lack of sympathy and sensitivity that Virginia Woolf continually associated with men.

"Ancestors" (1925) is almost a companion piece in that it presents a woman, Mrs. Vallance, with a similar aloof detachment from others. Her sense of superiority, as the title suggests, lies in the quality of her ancestors, particularly her accomplished father and beautiful, elegant mother. They surrounded themselves with beauty and with other intelligent and talented people so that in her childhood Mrs. Vallance heard "the most wonderful talk of her time" (175) and enjoyed the freedom of the Scottish countryside. She resents, therefore, the ugliness of London and the triviality of the chat at Mrs. Dalloway's party—talk of cricket and women's dresses. Even the drooping flowers remind her of her mother's passion for gardening. The whole party suggests the downward curve of her life since her parents' death: "how proud her father was of her, and how great he was, and how great her mother was, and how when she was with them . . . she had it in her to be anything. That if they had lived . . . and if that life could have gone on for ever, then Mrs. Vallance felt none of this . . . could have had any existence, and she would have been oh perfectly happy, perfectly good" (177).

It is difficult to read this story and not be reminded of Virginia Stephen's childhood and the family in which she grew up—an accomplished father surrounded with other men of distinction, and a mother whom Virginia adored.[19] Mrs. Vallance's passion for the Scottish countryside has its counterpart in young Virginia's love for the Stephens' summer home in Cornwall.[20] These autobiographical details, however, do not mean that in Mrs. Vallance Virginia Woolf was drawing a self-portrait. Rather, "Ancestors" is like "Phyllis and Rosamond" in depicting a life the author might have lived. Unlike Virginia Woolf, Mrs. Vallance dwells on the past, unable to free herself from a childhood so happy, secure, and fulfilling that the present holds nothing like it. But the fault is not so much the present as it is the lady herself, who has failed to capitalize on her education. The situation is much like that depicted in the early novel *Night and Day*, where Katherine Hilbery is given equally accomplished parents and the problem of deciding whom she will marry.[21] Whether Mrs. Vallance has married well we are not told, but the story does suggest the kind of empty snobbery that can result from a life of lost potential.

There are, of course, external threats to a woman's potential, and one of these is explored in "The Introduction" (1925). Joanne Trautmann Banks correctly identifies the theme of this story as "the endangered self."[22] The situation and manner in which this theme is worked out are typically Woolfian, for the story employs a number of ideas and techniques seen elsewhere in the short fiction. The central character and center of consciousness is Lily Everit, ill at ease, attending her first party. Like some of the other guests, she would prefer to remain inconspicuous, but Mrs. Dalloway, the perfect hostess, insists on introducing her to Bob Brinsley in the belief that the two young people, both lovers of Shelley, will find much in common. Lily's reluctance comes not just from shyness but from a desire to hang on to something precious—the memory of the high compliment paid to her earlier that day by a professor for her essay on Swift. The essay she regards as her true self; the visible exterior, so carefully prepared by her sister and the maid, is merely surface. Lily, like Mabel Waring in "The New Dress" and Sasha Latham in "A Summing Up," regards her appearance as a betrayal of her inner integrity.

The threat to Lily Everit's self comes not simply from having to mix socially with others but from the fact of having to meet a young man. In a society where a woman is regarded chiefly as an adornment to a successful male, Lily feels as if she is being degraded. We are back to the social milieu of "A Society," in which the female is threatened by the intimidating world of male accomplishments. To Lily these are symbolized by Westminster Abbey, Parliament, the telegraph. Ironically, all of this is missed by Mrs. Dalloway, who is "absurdly moved" (181) to introduce the young people and to play, as she fancies, the role of matchmaker. These two visions of the party—the one in which the self is completed by social interaction, the other in which the self is threatened—are a convenient shorthand by which the author can express the differences between two generations of women.

The situation itself is also a reflection of Virginia Woolf's own anxieties in similar circumstances. To cite but one instance: "My feeling is that excessive masculinity has to be guarded against; I mean young men do seem to me so selfish and assertive" (*Letters* 2:195). Bob Brinsley is just such a young man. His manner is so confident and condescending that Lily feels herself being pulled apart, as if she were a fly (again the comparison with Mabel Waring is instructive) and he a tormenting boy, tearing off her wings. But the attack, as she perceives it, is not simply personal. While being dragged from her corner to meet Brinsley, Lily recalls the freedom and delicious solitude of the woods and dreads "this regulated life, which fell like a yoke about her neck" (180). This same image recurs when Brinsley turns away from her and Lily feels the yoke of civilization fall from the sky and land crushingly on her neck (182). This civilization, she feels, depends on her (presumably as wife, mother, and ornament), yet like Eve expelled from the garden, she will have no part in shaping it.[23]

"The Introduction" is among the most successful of Virginia Woolf's stories, in part because of its extreme concentration and unity of construction. The story covers no more than a few minutes of time, yet in it we see the essence of a young woman's individual and social dilemma. The stories around it, of course, help to set its scene and mood; the character of Mrs. Dalloway, here portrayed as formidable and intimidating, comes ready-made. These devices aid in the distilling process, but the fire is provided by Woolf's style. Exactness of diction describes a part of her stylistic effects, the way in which a simple phrase like "benevolent and drastic" (178) can capture the contradictory impressions of Mrs. Dalloway, or a happy image—"Lily . . . might have been the wayward sailing boat curtseying in the wake of a steamer" (179)—can precisely convey both the visual and emotional situation. Equally important is the work each sentence does to hold in suspension, like a supersaturated solution, an excess of contrary and conflicting emotions and ideas:

> Looking out, Lily Everit instinctively hid that essay of hers, so ashamed was she now, so bewildered too, and on tiptoe nevertheless to adjust her focus and get into right proportions (the old having been shamefully wrong) these diminishing and expanding things (what could one call them? people—impressions of people's lives?) which seemed to menace and mount over her, to turn everything to water, leaving her only—for that she would not resign—the power to stand at bay. (179)

This is a single sentence, yet it seems to contain more information than most pages, its emphasis and balance precariously held by dashes and parentheses. In spite of its awkward look and complex structure, the sentence hurries forward, almost tumbles, with the swiftness of Lily's thought and the panic of the moment. This, in brief, is the quality of the whole story: vivid, exciting, complex. By conventional standards, nothing has happened, but a life and a society have been condensed to a moment.

"Together and Apart" (ca. 1925; publ. 1944) is also the record of a meeting brought about by Mrs. Dalloway. In this case the man and woman are middle-aged, she a Miss Anning, he a minor poet, Roderick Serle. In keeping with the ages of the principals, this story is longer, slower paced, and less intense than its predecessor, but also far more subtle. Whereas "The Introduction" deals in vivid conflicting emotions, "Together and Apart" concerns subtle shades of feeling. Just what these feelings are is difficult to say without oversimplifying the story. They can generally be described as the feelings of two people who have been introduced and who could be friends but who are temperamentally or perhaps temporarily unable to find a common bond, even though one exists. Wariness and indolence characterize Miss Anning, as she admits to herself. She is naturally shy and lacking energy and so needs to goad herself into making conversation. He is socially adept, used to attending parties, but outwardly melancholy and difficult. Their conversation consists of only half a dozen short speeches each; the rest of the story delves into the private feelings, reactions, and memories sparked by the conversation. The contrast, even clash, of these two interior monologues forms the material of the story.

The possibility of a bond between the two protagonists is created by Miss Anning's commonplace remark that twenty years ago she had met a Miss Serle in Canterbury. Whether this Miss Serle is related to Roderick we never learn, but Canterbury to him is more than a memory— it is the place that looms largest in his life and imagination. To her, also, it is something special, for she can remember to this day Miss Serle's comments about the thunder and the peculiar impression the city made upon her. But the common link that memory and Canterbury could forge is never made, even though for one brief instant there seems to be an unspoken communication between them. At this moment, Miss Anning could describe her feelings for Serle as love, yet because he does not respond in any way, let alone in kind, the moment passes. Seconds later they are interrupted by a third party, and the story ends.

If the tone of "The Introduction" is sharp and angry, the feeling engendered by "Together and Apart" is wistful regret. Here is a chance for two strangers to communicate, if not deeply, then at least at a level beyond the usual. Unknown to either of them, they share an experience of place and time that could afford each an opportunity to revive significant memories. Part of the reason for this lost opportunity is Serle's masculine arrogance, his feeling that this woman could not possibly understand what Canterbury has meant to him. Ironically, he has tried to express this indirectly in his poetry and failed. Indeed, he feels himself a failure, not having lived up to a tenth of his promise, and for this he blames his "extraordinary facility and responsiveness to talk" and his inability to "cut himself off utterly from society and the company of women" (185). For an instant he had felt that this woman could provide him, at the age of fifty, with a new beginning, but he fails to seize the opportunity. Smugness, for want of a better word, or perhaps an inability to risk something of himself, has prevented him from making the kind of human contact he believes he wants. Once again he will leave a party and return home "dissatisfied with his life, with himself, yawning, empty, capricious" (186).

"The Man Who Loved His Kind" (publ. 1944) was probably completed in 1925, a conclusion supported by the similarity of its main character to Charles Tansley of *To the Lighthouse* (1927). We might surmise that Prickett Ellis of the story is a more complete working out of Tansley than was possible in the novel. In the first part of the novel, Tansley is one of Mr. Ramsey's protégés, working on his dissertation. He is portrayed as abrasive, self-centered, and overly proud of his humble origins. In the second half, Lily Briscoe recalls hearing him speak during the war and thinks to herself: "He was preaching brotherly love. And all she felt was how could he love his kind who did not know one picture from another, who had stood behind her smoking shag ('five-pence an ounce, Miss Brisco') and making it his business to tell her women can't write, women can't paint."[24]

Like Lily Briscoe's characterization of Charles Tansley, "The Man Who Loved His Kind" seems perfectly clear at first, but the story becomes more complex and problematic on subsequent readings. It begins on the morning of Mrs. Dalloway's party when Richard Dalloway bumps into his old school friend Ellis and invites him to the party that night. Ellis regrets the invitation as soon as he has accepted it but attends anyway, feeling at first merely out of place and then by degrees angry at the wealth and frivolity of the party. He is a socialist lawyer, proud of his dedication to the poor and of his own self-denial; he allows himself only the cheapest tobacco and a brief vacation each year. The books in the Dalloways' library are almost a reproach to his ascetic life, and as he surveys the scene, resentment grows. "He did not feel this—that he loved humanity, that he paid only five pence an ounce for tobacco and loved nature—naturally and quietly. Each of these pleasures had been turned into a protest. He felt that these people whom he despised made him stand and deliver and justify himself" (191). In his desire for justification, he reflects on the events of that morning, when a couple whom he had represented without fee presented him with an inexpensive clock as a token of gratitude. Moments like these make his work worthwhile and give his life meaning.

As he is thinking these thoughts, Richard introduces Miss O'Keefe, who carries her own baggage of social conscience. That day she too had seen social injustice in the form of a poor woman and her children. Feeling impotent to change the system producing such poverty, she now appears arrogant and haughty. In the conversation that follows, Prickett Ellis attempts to justify himself to Miss O'Keefe by critizing the party and telling her of his morning's clients. She reacts bitterly to his self-righteous smugness and in turn criticizes him for being insensitive to beauty and nature. The story ends, "Hating each other, hating the whole houseful of people who had given them this painful, this disillusioning evening, these two lovers of their kind got up, and without a word parted forever" (194).

The sentence quoted above reflects the fact that Virginia Woolf originally titled the story "Lovers of Their Kind" (Dick, 298), a more appropriate title than the one the story now bears. The story's satire (if that is the right word) is not directed solely at Prickett Ellis, however unsavory he may be, but at an attitude Virginia Woolf found offensive, and this is held by Miss O'Keefe as well. It is not merely their pharisaical self-righteousness that is attacked, although this is certainly one of the story's targets, nor is the point of the story the heavy-handed irony of the last paragraph, in which two lovers of their kind are revealed as full of hatred. Important and obvious as these themes are, they do not express the heart of the story.

However offended we may be by Prickett Ellis's attitude toward the guests at the Dalloways' party, we cannot deny that he has a point— the world is full of injustice and inequities, and most of the people enjoying themselves at this get-together are the beneficiaries of that injustice. Their wealth and leisure are made possible by others' suffering. Miss O'Keefe's observations underscore the point, if it needs emphasis. If we glibly criticize Ellis and O'Keefe, therefore, we miss a vital element in the story's tension—the justice of Ellis's criticisms. The very fact that Virginia Woolf has chosen to interject these ideas into the party indicates her concern with this contrast. It is also relevant to note that the contrast between suffering and frivolity was one of the themes of "The Evening Party," already discussed. The conflict they feel is also one that she experienced throughout her adult life as the wife of Leonard Woolf, a tireless political agitator and reformer. Although she did not share Leonard's political interests, she could not pretend that politics was simply the arena of insensitive fools. Nevertheless, she found many of Leonard's friends dull and one-sided. A likely candidate for the model of Prickett Ellis is Sidney Webb, a long-time associate of Leonard's about whom Virginia wrote in her diary: "I've always quarrelled with the Webbs. You see Webb has a gigantic faculty for absorbing information. He could have gone to Oxford— found some flaw in the statutes—proved it to the examiners. But didn't go: only wanted to be in the right" (*Diary* 4:106). While writing *Mrs. Dalloway*, she complained of interruptions, particularly when the interloper was Sidney Webb: "And Sidney, however one may discount him beforehand, is always a feather bed on a hot night—ponderous, meritorious, stuffy" (*Diary* 2:190–91).

By contrast, Woolf's biographer writes: "Leonard steadily won her respect as a political speaker and as a champion of the Women's Co-operative movement. . . . She approved, too, his unpretentious manner with women."[25] These biographical notes and the context and tone of the story itself suggest that Virginia Woolf is attacking the manner more than the matter of Ellis's criticisms. His unease at the contrast between rich and poor may be justified, but his priggish manner and desire for public recognition are socially and morally offensive.

There is also a psychological level to this story that can easily be missed, and that is the motivation behind the anger expressed by both lovers of their kind. Woolf describes it in Ellis's case as follows: "Each of these pleasures [tobacco and a love of nature] had been turned into a protest" (191). In Miss O'Keefe's case, her anger arises from the fact that she was playing tennis while she saw the unfortunate woman and children. In other words, both are guilty of precisely the sin they claim to hate—of taking pleasure while others suffer. The party, with its easy luxury, enables them to feel superior to the others, but it also reminds them that there is no absolute division between themselves and the others, no pristine purity that they can claim. Theirs, too, are guilty pleasures, and from this arises their anger at the others and at one another.

"The Man Who Loved His Kind," therefore, is not the sophomoric exercise in exposing hypocrisy that it may first appear but a complex story that reaches to the roots of Virginia Woolf's own ambivalence about politics and social action.

"A Simple Melody" (1925?) is an unusual short story in that it depends heavily upon the others in the party sequence for its effects. This is so in part because it contrasts sharply in tone with all the preceding party stories: all of them are to some extent concerned with conflict, and in "The Man Who Loved His Kind" the tension has reached almost violent proportions. In this story, however, all is calm and repose. It takes the form of an interior monologue, almost an essay, tracing the thoughts of Mr. Carslake as he contemplates a painting of a Norfolk heath. The painting soothes Mr. Carslake and seems to him like a calm center in the noisy hubbub of the party. "It was as if a fiddler were playing a perfectly quiet old English song while people gambled and tumbled and swore, picked pockets, rescued the drowning, and did astonishing—but quite unnecessary—feats of skill" (195). Beyond this, he spends much of his time thinking how alike people are beneath their superficial differences, and he is certain that if he, Miss Merewether, and the Queen were walking together on this heath they would converse in a natural and easy way, finding points of commonality among themselves.

As Carslake thinks these thoughts, he sees Mabel Waring ("The New Dress") and notices her pretty dress as well as her agitated look. He also notes Stuart Elton ("Happiness") picking up the letter opener and the angry look on Prickett Ellis's face. All these people, he thinks, would find ease and common human bonds if they were out of London and with him on the Norfolk heath. Carslake is not a simple-minded romantic, however, for he acknowledges complexities in this simple notion. The permanence of the heath reminds him of the transitoriness of life; the image of a pond arouses a complex series of ideas on understanding as a human goal; the inconsistency of his own nature suggests that people may be as essentially divided as they are essentially alike. And beyond all of these ideas lies the basic problem of communicating thought, or even of separating it from emotion. Meanwhile, as Carslake is thinking these things, Miss Merewether is considering him, recalling his bachelor life with his mother, his reputation as a speaker, and his odd manners. The story concludes when he tells her an anecdote about his nephew and she thinks what an odd fellow he is.

From some points of view this is not a very successful story: it depends perhaps too much on others in the series and hence lacks the self-sufficiency of a good short story; its central character is unclearly presented, in spite of what we learn through the interior monologue; its movement is largely that of abstract thought, rendering it somewhat sterile and removed; even the author's attitude toward her character and the ideas he expresses is at best ambivalent—and what are we to make of Miss Merewether's dismissal of him as "a queer fish"?

In spite of these objections, "A Simple Melody" is fascinating reading, in part because of the complex relationship it bears to the other stories in the party sequence. A common theme in the stories from "A New Dress" through "The Man Who Loved His Kind" is the forces that separate people. Mabel Waring's extreme self-consciousness, Stuart Elton's self-sufficiency, Mrs. Vallance's inability to transcend her parents' accomplishments, Mr. Brinsley's cruelty to Lily Everit, Mr. Serle's reluctance to talk to Miss Anning, Prickett Ellis's callous pride. Mr. Carslake, by contrast, attempts to find the common humanity behind these apparent conflicts and differences; whether he is successful is less important than the fact of his trying. His view balances the others, even though it does not cancel them out. It puts their concerns into a different perspective, not necessarily in itself a truer perspective, but one that makes the stories collectively more true by making them more complex.

"A Simple Melody" helps the reader to see that social conflicts often have their roots in individual's internal conflicts. At the same time, it takes some of the urgency and sting from the intensity of the preceding stories; their themes are not trivialized but revealed as less earth-shaking than might otherwise be the case. As Mr. Carslake thinks to himself at one point, "Indeed, these parties on the heath do not annihilate difference, he thought; but he maintained . . . that the only differences . . . are fundamental differences."(197) "A Simple Melody" provides some ballast in what might otherwise be a very unstable social vessel.

Another connection between "A Simple Melody" and the other stories is the problem of communication. Repeatedly this idea has appeared, from Mabel Waring's suspicion that all compliments on her dress were really criticisms to the unnecessary antagonism between Prickett Ellis and Miss O'Keefe. George Carslake looks not only at the phenomenon itself but also at its root causes, recognizing one of them—like the causes of social strife—as beginning within the individual. At one point he realizes that some of his ideas can be thought but not expressed because once expressed they sound like sentimental twaddle. At another point he sees that part of the difficulty lies in the way language has been abused: "His thoughts could not find any pure new words which had never been ruffled and creased and had the starch taken out of them by others' use" (197).

Perhaps these are the reasons that Carslake returns regularly to non-verbal communication, to the painting that triggered these ideas and to the simple melody that both harmonizes and disturbs. Art has a unity that people and society lack. But Carslake is not satisfied with these relatively simple observations. He forces himself to consider an alternate hypothesis, that there is something endemic in society and even individuals that makes people strive and contest against one another, like fish in a net. In the end, he sees no reconciliation of these opposites but only a paradox: that people both oppress and stimulate one another at the same time. It is only on the heath that they can move in harmony.

This is the complex interplay of ideas that makes "A Simple Melody" compelling reading. Like "The Mark on the Wall" it pulls us along by the force of its ideas, which again serve as the actions in a plot. And also like "The Mark on the Wall," there is the attraction of Woolf's style. It is simpler, plainer, and less breathless than in the earlier story, but also more serviceable. One habit retained from the earlier period is that of suspending important qualifiers between dashes, but in other respects the style is smoother and more polished. The meditative quality of the story also enables the writer to develop three points of interest as unifiers of Carslake's thought. These are the painting, the simple melody, and water. The functions of the first two have already been explained; they are unified works of art that contrast with the disruptive tendencies of society. Water first appears as a pond representing understanding, an earthly alternative to the idea of heaven as popularly depicted, then becomes a pool out of which his ideas bubble. From this it becomes a reservoir in which human "creatures" live, its surface ruffled by the simple melody. This in turn leads to the fish image noted above and its final manifestation—a vision in which the partygoers "swam side by side in the greatest comfort" (200). Water, therefore, becomes the unifying force uniting art, society, nature, and understanding. Here it is used as an idea rather than as a metaphor or symbol, a link between the natural and the artificial. As such it is not entirely satisfactory, reflecting the unsolvable riddle that Carslake has posed himself. He does not solve his problem, and he remains "a queer fish" in the eyes of Miss Merewether—another indication that the harmony he seeks is not to be found in society. Again, as in "The Mark on the Wall," the point is not the solution to the problem but the process of thinking through alternatives.

It is tempting to take literally the title of the last story in the party sequence, "A Summing Up" (publ. 1944), and to regard it as Virginia Woolf's last word on the themes raised in the previous stories. In some respects this is a valid approach, but it should not be pushed too far, for while some of the issues raised can in a sense be summarized they cannot be and are not resolved.

The story centers on Sasha Latham, whom Virginia Woolf describes as tall and attractive, exuding confidence but feeling inadequate—a description that in many ways could apply to the author herself. She is with her old friend Bertram Pritchard, who leads her into the cool and peace of the Dalloways' garden. Pritchard is depicted as an able civil servant with a genius for conversation: "There was a sound in his voice, some accent or emphasis, some lustre in the incongruity of his ideas, some emanation from his round chubby brown face and robin redbreasts's figure, something immaterial, unseizable, which existed and flourished and made itself felt independently of his words, indeed, often in opposition to them" (202). He is almost certainly modelled on Desmond MacCarthy, the most promising of the Bloomsbury set, who never lived up to his great potential in part because his gift was not for writing but for conversation. As Pritchard rattles on, Mrs. Latham's thoughts wander. Her first thoughts are that Mrs. Dalloway's party is an instance of the greatness of civilization. The house, the city of London humming around it, and the people gathered here in their evening clothes to entertain and be entertained seem to her a high achievement of civilization. A tree standing in the garden and a barrel against the house seem suffused in pure gold.

These thoughts are interrupted by Bertram's insistence that they explore the garden. Looking over the garden wall at London, Mrs. Latham suddenly has a vision of the city as a boot or a bucket. Her glittering view of the party is abruptly reversed: "There they sat again, looking at the same house, the same tree, the same barrel; only having looked over the wall and had a glimpse of the bucket, or rather of London going its way unconcernedly, Sasha could no longer spray over the world that cloud of gold" (204). The party, the Dalloways' house, and the people become ordinary, prosaic; and like George Carslake in the previous story, Mrs. Latham asks herself which of the two views is true. The answer comes to her not by logic but from the appearance of the tree and the fact that her soul seems to perch in it like a widow bird. At just that instant, she hears an unidentified scream and sees her soul fly away like a frightened bird.

These two visions, the one of society and civilization as a high attainment, the other of these as dull and indifferent, continue but do not resolve the problems posed in earlier stories. Moreover, Mrs. Latham's vision of the soul as a lone bird suggests that the individual is always solitary, isolated. In this way, the story sums up but does not resolve the conflicts it and the other stories pose, for the conflicts cannot be settled. Each person at the party has felt these tensions to one degree or another, manifested the problems in one way or another. The purpose of the stories has not been to settle unresolvable quarrels but to explore their manifestations in different situations and psyches. As in so many of her stories, Virginia Woolf is ultimately less interested in social and political ideas than she is in states of consciousness.

The party is a unifying device enabling Woolf to examine people of various kinds in a single situation and a convenient way to bring together a number of social types and ranks. Her own ambivalence about parties and her long experience with them provided a wealth of firsthand material to incorporate into the stories and also perhaps some special motivation for focusing particularly on women. In style and form, they are not obviously experimental, but each presented a challenge in getting quickly inside a character or characters and to explore the thoughts and feeling found there. Individually, the stories may not strike the reader as great short fiction, but collectively they represent a considerable achievement in a rarely practiced and seldom analyzed form—the story sequence. The lessons learned in these stories would be put to good use in *Mrs. Dalloway* and *To the Lighthouse*.

At two different times during the 1920s, Virginia Woolf briefly put aside her serious writing to produce stories for children. Susan Dick places the date of "Nurse Lugton's Curtain" at 1924 and concludes on the basis of Leonard Woolf's testimony that it was written for Ann Stephen, Virginia Woolf's niece (Dick, 296). "The Widow and the Parrot: A True Story" cannot be dated precisely, but seems like its companion piece to have been written for the Bell children in the 1920s (Dick, 296). Although both are whimsical and light-hearted, each shows a different side of Virginia Woolf's imagination and a different aspect of her style in the lighter vein.

"Nurse Lugton's Curtain" is pure fantasy. When Nurse Lugton falls asleep over the curtain she is sewing for Mrs. Jasper, the figures on the blue material come to life. The animals graze or go down to the lake for a drink; the people in the town go quickly about their business, knowing that at any time the ogress Lugton may awaken and charm them back into immobility. All too soon, a fly disturbs Lugton's sleep and she does wake up, whereupon all the activity in the curtain material ceases and Lugton resumes sewing. There is nothing remarkable in this momentary fancy: the idea of inanimate things coming to life while humans sleep is hardly original with Virginia Woolf. The story derives its charm from the vitality of the writing, which is simple and clear without being childish. The combination of childlike fantasy with long, almost breathless sentences and mature diction may remind the reader of Laurent de Brunhoff's stories of Babar the elephant. There is also the same air of delightful innocence in the presentation, and for the children, of course, the idea of seeing an old nurse as an ogress provides just the right touch of naughtiness.

"The Widow and the Parrot: A True Story" is in the tradition folklorists would identify as the "helpful animal" type. Using local features of the Rodmell area where the Bells lived, Virginia Woolf constructs a story about an old widow, Mrs. Gage, who inherits a house and £3,000 from her miserly brother Joseph. The trouble is that when she arrives to claim her legacy, she finds the house and its furnishings worthless and the money alluded to in the will missing. The only thing of value left is a large grey parrot named James, whose single utterance is "Not at home!" Returning late from the lawyers' office, Mrs. Gage finds herself lost and unable to cross the Ouse River to reach her brother's house. She is saved by a great light that suddenly flares and that proves to be her brother's house on fire. Her main concern is for the parrot, but all appears lost. She is taken in by a neighbor and put to bed. Later that night, James the parrot pecks on her window and leads her back to the charred house, where his odd way of tapping on the kitchen bricks eventually leads Mrs. Gage to uncover exactly three thousand gold sovereigns. The next day she returns to her village in Yorkshire where she lives a long and happy life with James.

Although there is nothing distinguished about this story, it shows that its author was perfectly capable of producing fiction of the conventional type when the occasion demanded. Here the occasion is provided by her sister's children, who must have been enthralled by the use of the local landscape and by the liveliness of the story. Mrs. Gage is an appealing widow, with a fondness for animals and a gentle nature. Her deceased brother is a worthy villain. The plot is skillfully constructed, with Mrs. Gage's fortunes seeming to decline unfairly, even as they are in fact ascending with appropriate poetic justice. Children, who are inclined to think of animals as superior to adults, no doubt find Mrs. Gage's devotion to her dog and parrot as well worthy of her reward. The whimsical tone of the story and its sprightly style remind the reader of similar though more accomplished stories by Virginia Woolf's contemporary and acquaintance, Sylvia Townsend Warner. It is not unusual for great writers to produce, almost offhandedly, excellent writing for children: Oscar Wilde and T. S. Eliot come readily to mind. Virginia Woolf's children's stories are not of this caliber, but they show a side to her nature that seldom appears in her serious fiction. In these light-hearted pieces we can see her delight in humor and fancy, qualities that often appear in her letters to the children for whom these stories were written but that we seldom associate with the high priestess of Bloomsbury.

Four additional stories produced during this middle period do not fit either the party sequence or the children's stories discussed above. Two of these, "Moments of Being: 'Slater's Pins Have No Points'" (1926) and "The Lady in the Looking-Glass: A Reflection" (1929), are very similar in manner and style to "An Unwritten Novel." Like their predecessor, these two stories depict attempts by one person to understand another by interpreting exterior clues. "Moments of Being" is perhaps the most concentrated and complex of Woolf's short stories. Though it occupies six pages of small print in the *Complete Shorter Fiction*, it concerns perhaps two minutes of "real time." It opens with Miss Craye's eccentric remark, "'Slater's pins have no points—don't you always find that?'" (209), occasioned by the fact that the carnation has fallen from Fanny Wilmot's dress. Miss Craye, an elderly music teacher, has been playing Bach for her favorite pupil Fanny. The remark triggers a complex train of thought by Fanny Wilmot in which she pieces together from heard and observed clues the life of Miss Craye as she imagines it, focusing particularly on the reasons that Miss Craye never married. At the end, when the offending pin has been found, Fanny's conjectures are jolted when Miss Craye kisses her. The clear implication is that Miss Craye is a lesbian.

We can trace the genesis of "Moments of Being" with unusual precision to a diary entry dated 5 September 1926.

> As usual, side stories are sprouting in great variety as I wind this up: a book of characters; the whole string being pulled out from some simple sentence, like Clara Pater's, "Don't you find that Barker's pins have no points to them?" I think I can spin out all their entrails this way; but it is hopelessly undramatic. It is all in oration obliqua. Not quite all; for I have a few direct sentences. (*Diary* 3:106)

Clara Pater was Virginia Woolf's first tutor in Greek, and she and the second tutor, Janet Case, may have supplied the outline of the character of the music teacher, Miss Craye, minus the lesbianism. There can be no doubt that lesbianism is intended at the ending, however, for the author twice refers to it in letters to Vita Sackville-West as her "Sapphist" story for the Americans (*Letters* 3:396, 431).

The effect of Miss Craye's observation, "Slater's pins have no points," is to awaken suddenly in Fanny Wilmot a whole new series of questions about her piano teacher. This is apparently the first time Fanny has thought of her teacher as an ordinary person, with a life like anyone else's. She surmises, in fact, that Miss Craye's purpose in the remark is to "break the pane of glass which separated them [i.e., the Crayes] from other people" (210). Thus she recalls the words of Miss Kingston, the school principal, describing Miss Craye's life with her brother, a famous archaeologist. Miss Craye's comment about Slater's pins, Miss Kingston's background information about the Craye family, and a few incidental observations constitute the "facts" Miss Wilmot has to work with in constructing her portrait of Miss Craye. The rest is supplied by imagination, supposition, and a curious tone in Miss Kingston's voice suggesting that there is something "odd" or "queer" in Miss Craye (210). This phrase takes on its meaning at the end of the story; at the outset it means nothing more to Miss Wilmot than eccentricity and, as she sees Miss Craye holding the carnation that has fallen from her dress, "perpetual frustration" (211).

These clues apparently strike more deeply than Miss Wilmot realizes at the instant, for her next question, and the one she pursues throughout the rest of the story, is why Miss Craye never married. She recalls in particular two remarks of Miss Craye's about men, one to the effect that the only use of men is to protect women and the other that men are ogres. Around these Miss Wilmot spins imaginary incidents of courtship and proposals spurned, and of a life given meaning by Miss Craye's battles against the headaches that have plagued her for years. Surely Miss Craye is lonely. But, no, there is Miss Craye looking radiant, and for a moment the whole of Miss Craye's life seems clear. At this moment, Miss Craye kisses Julia—not just kisses but "possesses" her. The story falls into place with a firm click.

It is tempting to analyze this story from a Freudian perspective and to see it as an unconscious portrait of frustration and repressed lesbianism through the eyes of a girl too young and inexperienced to know the full meaning of what she says about her teacher. In such a reading, Slater's pins would be phallic symbols and Miss Craye's comment a thinly veiled criticism of men in general. The approach might be vindicated by noting that the Hogarth Press had published Freud in England.[26]

Although the Freudian elements of the story are clear, focusing on them here would be incongruous with this essay's goal of examining other elements in Virginia Woolf's short fiction. For our purposes, it is more to the point to note that the story is another attempt to explore the possibility of one person's knowing another. In this instance, both Miss Wilmot and the reader have more solid information than in "An Unwritten Novel," but the facts are complicated by the naive narrator. Even at the end of the story it is not clear that Miss Wilmot understands fully the implications of the kiss, though to readers they seem clear enough. This, in turn, calls into question the life Miss Wilmot has imagined for Miss Craye: to what extent can we trust her reconstructions of other events? The answer, of course, is that we cannot trust them at all, at least not to tell us anything about Miss Craye. What they do reveal is their inventor, Miss Wilmot, the favorite pupil honored by her teacher and jolted by an offhand remark into an awareness of her as a person. The would-be novelist in "The Unwritten Novel" revealed an imagination colored by the clichés of popular fiction. Miss Wilmot might be accused of relying too much on romantic renunciation. She sees her teacher as interested chiefly in maintaining her independence and recognizes both the advantages and disadvantages of that decision. To her Miss Craye is something of an heroic figure, though a heroine of quite ordinary proportions and accomplishments. Certainly she sees her spinsterhood as a matter of choice and preference.

The ironic reversal at the end of the story does more than reveal Miss Wilmot's naiveté and more than call into question our ability to know another person. It raises the whole question of character formation, of the extent to which we can choose to be what we are. Miss Wilmot believes that her teacher has chosen a way of life that is congenial to her; what the story dramatizes is the unknown forces that may shape character without our being aware. "Moments of Being" is thus a tour de force of Woolf's "undramatic" method. From an apparent hodgepodge of materials she has distilled an interior monologue of seemingly random associations that turn out in the end to illuminate both the observer and the observed. Manner and message are joined in a perfect whole.

Like "Moments of Being," "The Lady in the Looking-Glass: A Reflection" (1929) derives from a specific incident recorded in the diary: "One of these days, though, I shall sketch here, like a grand historical picture, the outlines of all my friends. . . . It might be a most amusing book. The question is how to do it. . . . How many little stories come into my head. For instance: Ethel Sands not looking at her letters. What this implies. One might write a book of short significant separate scenes. She did not open her letters" (*Diary* 3:156–57).

The story that emerged from this impulse is as problematic as the other two of the same type. It is narrated by a guest, presumably a female, of Isabella Tyson, whom the narrator describes as a spinster of fifty-five or sixty, rich, elegant, cultivated, and well-traveled. The guest/narrator is left in the drawing room to wait as Isabella goes into the garden. Left alone, the narrator is free to reflect on Isabella, and in so doing she sets up two modes of perception, the one direct, the other what is reflected in the mirror. Interestingly, the mirror provides a glimpse at reality that direct observation does not. The opening and closing sentences of the story assert that people should not hang mirrors "any more than they should leave open cheque books or letters confessing some hideous crime" (215). Direct observation, by contrast, provides information that is merely fleeting and transient: "But, outside, the looking-glass reflected the hall table, the sunflowers, the garden path so accurately and so fixedly that they seemed held there in their reality unescapably. It was a strange contrast—all changing here, all stillness there" (215). The narrator vows to get to the truth about Isabella Tyson and so will use the most subtle tool available—imagination—for the facts, such as they are, tell nothing. This reverie is briefly interrupted when the postman delivers the mail, and suddenly it seems to the narrator that to know what is in these letters would be to know Isabella completely. As Isabella returns from the garden, the mirror catches her reflection and reveals her by degrees in ways that conform to the facts. But when she stops to read her letters, which turn out to be all bills, the vision is startling: "Here was the woman herself. She stood naked in that pitiless light. And there was nothing. Isabella was perfectly empty. She had no thoughts. She had no friends. She cared for nobody" (219).

If we can trust the narrator and the ending, we have here the only story in which the narrator is able to pierce the barrier of external reality and discover something essential about her subject. Why is this narrator able to succeed where Fanny Wilmot and the narrator of "An Unwritten Novel" were not? The answer is the mirror, for it does more than reflect; it also composes and holds. When the postman brings the letters, for instance, the mirror image is momentarily disturbed. "There they lay on the marble-topped table, all dripping with light and colour at first and crude and unabsorbed. And then it was strange to see how they were drawn in and arranged and composed and made part of the picture and granted that stillness and immortality which the looking-glass conferred" (217). The mirror, in other words, is art.

The narrator, using only her imagination and the facts available to her, is unable to get any closer to the truth than the previous narrators. What she imagines about Isabella in the garden, for example, is similar to what the other narrators thought about their subjects—it is plausible and interesting enough, but there is no way to verify it. By some unexplained alchemy, the mirror transcends the flux of life: "Meanwhile, since all the doors and windows were open in the heat, there was a perpetual sighing and ceasing sound, the voice of the transient and the perishing, it seemed, coming and going like human breath, while in the looking-glass things had ceased to breathe and lay still in the trance of immortality" (215–16).

Taking the statements about the mirror together, we can see that the dichotomy is not between fact and imagination simply, but between life and art. Life is exactly this—alive—hence a part of the world of flux and change that makes some kinds of knowledge difficult if not impossible. The world of art, by contrast, is fixed. It is the same contrast Mr. Carslake noted in "A Simple Melody." It is not simply that facts need to be illumined by imagination, for all three narrators have done exactly that. Rather, until fact and imagination are unified into a stable work of art the subject remains elusive, changing, quixotic. Art holds the object, in this case Isabella Tyson, at least for a moment of revelation. Whether we are to regard the mirrors' revelation as *the* truth about Isabella or merely *a* truth remains an open question. The latter seems more likely, given Virginia Woolf's continued striving after form and method in her short and long fiction. In any event, "The Lady in the Looking-Glass" is the last of three similar stories and thus seems to represent Virginia Woolf's last fictional statement of the problem until "The Shooting Party" (1938), where it receives just a slight twist in the direction indicated by her treatment of it here.

After the publication of "Moments of Being" and "Lady in the Looking-Glass" in 1929, Virginia Woolf published no short fiction until "The Duchess and the Jeweller" in 1938. These nine years were extremely productive in other forms, however, yielding her novels *The Waves* (1931) and *The Years* (1937), the second collection of *Common Reader* essays (1932), and the biography *Flush* (1933). These years were productive in another sense, too, for Virginia Woolf's fame rose with each new book, and sales grew correspondingly. In fact, *The Years* became a bestseller in America, and royalties from U. S. sales alone came to well over $5,000—a substantial sum in the days just before World War II (*Letters* 6:130, 202). These facts may help explain why she devoted relatively little time to the short story, producing during this period only seven stories, none of which was published in her lifetime, and none of which commands a great deal of interest. Nevertheless, we can see in these attempts her continued experimentation with form and technique.

"The Fascination of the Pool" (1929) is in many ways a return to the manner of "The Mark on the Wall," "Kew Gardens," and "Blue and Green." It is almost an essay rather than a story, being a meditation on a farm pond in whose surface presently are reflected the white farm house and the for sale sign. The writer fancies that the pool holds the memories of those who have sat beside it. From these she draws three: a soldier who drank from it in 1851, the year of the Great Exhibition; a girl who hid with her lover in the rushes during the revolution in the 1660s before committing suicide; a boy who fished in the pond for a giant carp. Beneath these are other voices and memories that seem to want to rise to the surface bringing "our thoughts and longings and questions and confessions and disillusions into the light of day" (211), but somehow they always slip back into the pool. Perhaps, the writer muses, it is to hear these that we sit fascinated by the sides of pools.

"Three Pictures" (1929) was first published in the collection of essays *The Death of the Moth* (1942), which provides some idea of its ambiguity of form. The title is descriptive, for the story consists of three verbal sketches, the first describing an idyllic scene in which a sailor returns to his wife and children after months at sea. The scene is deliberately sweet and sentimental, as if the author were consciously evoking a rural set-piece. The second picture is more aural than visual, describing a woman's scream in the middle of a dark night. There is no apparent connection between this picture and the first. The third provides the connection and comes directly from an experience recorded in Virginia Woolf's diary of 4 September 1927. On that day, she had seen the local gravedigger at Rodmell digging a grave for the son of the local publican, a sailor. What is striking about the description in both the diary and the story is the stark contrast between the happy gravedigger and his family, picnicking on the mound of dirt beside the grave, and the solemnity of the occasion itself. The author makes no comment on the scenes but allows them to suggest their own significance to the reader. The style in these scenes, as in "The Fascination of the Pool," is simple and pictorial, as if Virginia Woolf were experimenting in word painting and atmosphere. It is a step in the direction of the style of *The Years* and the later stories.

The rest of the stories in this group are experimental character sketches. Some were undoubtedly written for a projected series of twelve "illustrated incidents" that were planned as a joint project by Virginia and her sister, Vanessa Bell, to be published by the Hogarth Press (*Diary* 5:58–61). The project was never completed, but since Woolf alludes to some sketches already on hand and mentions writing others, Susan Dick postulates that those labelled "Portraits" and the sketch entitled "Uncle Vanya" were probably intended for this booklet, while the others are independent (Dick, 300).

"Scenes from the Life of A British Naval Officer" (1931?) and "Miss Pryme" (undated) appear to be deliberate caricatures, an odd exercise for a writer who strove mightily to capture people and experiences in all their complexity. The naval captain is depicted with two sets of images, one describing him as an idol carved from dark wood, the other as a robot, doing everything in precise mechanical moves. The style in this sketch is appropriately crisp and sharp, with unusually short, pointed sentences. There is none of the suggestive ambiguity of Woolf's usual style, but a clipped masculine assertiveness that reinforces the message of the sketch. This is not a man but a robot, a machine of which other machines are mere extensions. The style of "Miss Pryme" is less severe, but the intent is much the same. The name Pryme suggests the smug self-righteousness of the character, who moves from Wimbledon to the village of Rusham for the purpose of "doing good" as she understands it. This consists of "catching people doing what they should not do" (229), like the lax rector who sneaks out in the middle of Sunday service for a smoke, and of performing a host of charitable acts, from repairing the church to tending the dying. What is satirized here, of course, is not the desire to do good works but the spirit in which these are done, more as exercises in self-congratulation than as humble works of charity. Both of these sketches are sharply etched and acerbic, aimed more at ridicule than understanding.

"Ode Written Partly in Prose on Seeing the Name of Cutbush Above a Butcher's Shop in Pentonville" (1934) is even more uncharacteristic, in that it is written in a sort of free verse. It tells the story of John Cutbush, a young man of romantic yearnings, who decides to become a butcher rather than a florist and leads thereafter a humdrum life, at first reasonably successful in business, later losing customers to more aggressive competitors. The difficulty here is in assessing the author's tone: is she sympathetic toward the boy whose dreams are squelched by the limited visions of his parents and the need to support a family, or is she lampooning middle-class materialism? The last line of the piece, in which the author "salutes" Cutbush, appears to support a sympathetic reading. Even so, there remains an unsavory whiff of condescension in this depiction of sad futility.

The eight short sketches collected under the title "Portraits" are similar in spirit to the caricatures of the naval captain and Miss Pryme, but they are on the whole wittier and more complex in structure and style. The subjects are varied—a French couple waiting for lunch, a mother and her son, a socialite, an aesthete, and a pretentious middle-brow, among others. Not all the portraits are satirical, but the attempt is less to capture an individual than to portray a social type. They are similar in spirit to the characters of Addison and Steele, after the manner of Theophrastus. The purpose seems to be to call the reader's attention to aspects of human behavior and to shock him or her into recognition by the highlighting of manners, speech patterns, and habits of thought. Something of their method may be indicated by "Uncle Vanya," the separately titled piece. A couple is watching the last act of Chekhov's play. The girl (as she is called) at first credits the Russians with seeing through everything, but as the last lines of the play are presented, she turns to her companion and reassuringly accuses Russian writers of being "morbid." These easy, automatic, and shallow responses to he play are intended as exemplars of a Philistine approach to art.

The striking thing about these experiments is that they appear to represent a regression rather than a progression in technique. It is as if Virginia Woolf were experimenting with ways to simplify her approach to character, after she had spent most of a lifetime attempting to capture its complexity. As we shall see in the following section, this is indeed the direction in which her work was moving—away from the experimental and modernist toward something far more traditional.

Advancing into Tradition

When Virginia Woolf returned to writing and publishing short stories late in 1937, she apparently did so from motives that were as much monetary as artistic. As noted above, she was at the height of her fame with the reading public and was enjoying the income her books were earning. She was not by any means greedy, but she enjoyed the freedom that a comfortable income conferred, as well as the pleasure of buying nice things. As she recorded in her diary ten years previously, when *Orlando* was selling briskly: "Yesterday I spent 15/- on a steel brooch. I spent £3 on a mother of pearl necklace—& I haven't bought a jewel for 20 years perhaps! I have carpeted the dining room—and so on. . . . (For part of my misery was the perpetual limitation of everything; no chairs, or beds, no comfort, no beauty; & no freedom to move: all of which I determined there & then to win)" (*Diary* 3:212). By 1937 she had not only learned to appreciate money but to bargain a bit with editors and publishers for what she deemed a fair price for her work (e.g., *Letters* 6:110).

"The Duchess and the Jeweller" (publ. 1938) apparently began as one of the caricatures for the never-completed volume she planned to publish with Vanessa Bell (Dick, 301–2), but it was revived when *Harper's Bazaar* in America asked her specifically for a story, offering £200 (*Letters* 6:157–59). As Susan Dick has shown in her analysis of the story's several drafts (302), it began as a study of a Jew. The story's negative portrayal, however, led New York literary agent Jacques Chambrun to advise removing the racial overtones. This was eventually done, and the story was thus acceptable for publication in America. On the surface, these facts suggest that the story was written solely for its commercial potential, but this is not the case. In the privacy of her diary, Virginia Woolf wrote: "This morning I had a moment of the old rapture—think of it!—over copying The Duchess & the Jeweller, for Chambrun NY. I had to send a synopsis. I expect he'll regret the synopsis. But there was the old excitement, even in that little extravagant flash—more than in criticism I think" (*Diary* 5:107).

Whatever the exact mixture of motives behind it, "The Duchess and

the Jeweller" is by all measures the most conventional of Virginia
Woolf's stories to this point, with the exception of the "The Widow
and the Parrot," written for children. The first part of the story describes the rich furnishings of Oliver Bacon, London's most successful
jeweller, and outlines his rise from street urchin to successful mer-
chant. For all of his success, however, Bacon feels that his life is lacking something. That something becomes clear at his office, where he
receives the Duchess of Lambourne and buys from her for £20,000 a
pearl necklace he suspects is paste—because the Duchess holds before
him an implied promise of her daughter, who represents social prestige
and acceptance. The ironies of the story are rather obvious, almost
heavy-handed, as is the portrait of Oliver Bacon, who is described
throughout unflatteringly: "Imagine a giant hog in a pasture rich with
truffles; after unearthing this truffle and that, still it smells a bigger, a
blacker truffle under the ground further off. So Oliver snuffed always
in the rich earth of Mayfair another truffle, a blacker, a bigger further
off" (243).

The appeals of this story are almost entirely those of slick magazine
fiction. Both the duchess and the jeweller are flat characters—he
driven by greed and social aspirations, she by gambling debts. Her
willingness to barter her daughter is as ignoble as his desire to purchase
her. Each is given a slight saving grace to prevent the portraits from
being entirely one-sided: he has a touching affection for his late
mother, and she an almost engaging wiliness in bargaining with the
jeweller. The story is skillfully constructed, and there are occasional
stylistic flashes that raise the story above the merely commercial level.
Nonetheless, "The Duchess and the Jeweller" is hardly among Virginia Woolf's enduring fictions.

Like "The Duchess and the Jeweller," "The Shooting Party" (1938)
was commissioned by New York agent Jacques Chambrun and sold to
Harper's Bazaar for $1,000 (*Diary* 5:107). It also resembles the former
story in origin, for it too began as one of the proposed caricatures for
the "Faces and Voices" project. As Susan Dick has shown, this story
was also reworked considerably into its present form; in particular, the
opening and closing paragraphs that provide the framework for the
story were added later (302), and this is the change that gives the story
much of its interest. With the addition of the frame story, "The Shooting Party" resembles "An Unwritten Novel" in describing a train passenger for whom the narrator creates a life. The woman observed is
identified partly by the initials M. M. on her suitcase; the narrator calls

her Milly Masters. By her dress and the fact that she has a brace of pheasants in addition to the suitcase, the narrator infers that she is a housekeeper on a large estate where a hunting party has just occurred. The main story is presented as Milly Masters's recollection of the weekend.

Two very old women, Miss Antonia and Miss Rashleigh, eat a lunch of roast pheasant while the hunt rages outside. Their conversation alludes to their declining aristocratic family that made its fortunes plundering South America and is now represented only by themselves and the aging squire. The house is decaying around them. After lunch, they savor their wine and give the bird carcass to the old spaniel. The squire comes in from the hunt, together with three dogs who attack the spaniel. In an attempt to break up the dogs, the squire lashes out with his whip, accidentally striking Miss Rashleigh's cheek and causing furniture and pictures to fall. The story then shifts back to the railway carriage, where Milly Masters is twice more described, once as a "handsome, if elderly . . . well-dressed, if rather shabby woman" (254) whose eyes reflect the memory of the story just told. But in the last paragraph, with her eyes closed, she seems just an ordinary woman on an errand, "But did she, all the same, as she opened the carriage door and stepped out, murmur, 'Chk. Chk.' as she passed?" (254).

The sound "Chk. Chk." is important because it provides the link between Milly Masters and the great house; it is the sound she made at the beginning of the story and the same one Miss Antonia makes as she sews, waiting for lunch. It also points to the central problem of interpretation, the validity of the main story itself. This is not, however, quite the same problem as was posed in earlier stories, that of the accuracy of the imagination. The narrator here is not, evidently, a fellow passenger in the train, but a nearly omniscient observer. If "nearly omniscient" seems a contradiction, it is one necessitated by the ambiguous stance of the narrator. In the first paragraph, she mentions Milly and three other passengers, and in describing Milly's thoughts and status repeatedly uses the word "must" rather than "might": "Since she was telling over the story she must have been a guest there" (248). This sentence and others in this paragraph suggest that the main story itself is not in question, only how Milly Masters came to be in possession of it. This remains the point of view until the last paragraph, where suddenly the narrator's view of Milly Masters seems to alter, calling into question the assumptions about her identity that had been made throughout the story. The effect is similar to that created by

Hawthorne at the end of "Young Goodman Brown," where he asks if Brown's experience in the woods had merely been a dream. Here, however, the ambiguity seems to muddle rather than enrich the main narrative.

The events in the main story are clear enough, as is their interpretation. The theme of the story is violence, more specifically, "He who lives by the sword shall perish by the sword." The pheasant hunt itself, of course, is violent enough, as bird after bird falls before the hunters' guns. The more important violence is in the family history—the pillaging of South America, the death of the family's heirs in riding and hunting accidents, the seduction of local girls, including Milly Masters, whose son, the nearest claimant to the family fortune by blood, cleans the village church. Along with the decline of the family has come the decay of the house and the victimization of Miss Antonia and Miss Rashleigh, both of whom are described in images that recall the dead pheasants. Their eyes are red or blue, or are like pebbles, as are the pheasants', and "their hands gripped their hands like the claws of dead birds gripping nothing" (253). The theme of the hunter hunted is paralleled in the dog fight.

In its manner of telling and in its themes of violence and decay, "The Shooting Party" is among Virginia Woolf's finest stories. The descriptions are sharp and telling. Much of the story is as vivid as this: "Out of the King's Ride the pheasants were being driven across the noses of the guns. Up they spurted from the underwood like heavy rockets, reddish purple rockets, and as they rose the guns cracked in order, eagerly, sharply, as if a line of dogs had suddenly barked. Tufts of white smoke held together for a moment; then gently solved themselves, faded, and dispersed" (249). Here, the liveliness of the description of the pheasants and the image of the guns as dogs give the passage a particular richness. Many other such could be cited. The problem with the story remains its point of view. Perhaps the mystery created by the final paragraph gives the story an added dimension, but it is also likely that in her desire to meet a deadline Virginia Woolf allowed herself to be a bit too clever and hence created rather than solved a problem.

Lyndall Gordon, who calls "Lappin and Lapinova" (publ. 1939) Virginia Woolf's "best story," has established its autobiographical basis.[27] In "Lappin and Lapinova" Rosalind is married to Ernest Thorburn and wonders from the beginning whether she can ever get used to his first name or to the idea of being married at all. On their honeymoon, she notices a slight resemblance between Ernest and a rabbit and hence dubs him King Lappin, king and lawgiver to the rabbits. He enjoys this honor, and eventually the game leads to her becoming Lapinova, a white hare and Lappin's queen. This shared fantasy makes them feel special and intimate, but it has a practical function, too, for on occasions when Rosalind feels excluded, as she does during her in-laws' golden anniversary celebration, the game provides a refuge. Eventually, however, they lose hold of this fancy, until one day even Rosalind cannot revive Lapinova in her imagination. That evening when Ernest returns from work, Rosalind says that Lapinova has died. He agrees: "'Caught in a trap,' he said, 'killed,' and sat down and read the newspaper. So that was the end of that marriage" (262).

The impetus for this story may well have come from a moment recorded by Virginia Woolf in a letter to Vanessa Bell, who had invited Virginia to join her in Cassis: "Its an awful confession—if I weren't so hurried I would conceal it; but the fact is we are so unhappy apart that I cant come. That's the worst failure imaginable—that marriage, as I suddenly for the first time realized walking in the Square, reduces one to damnable servility. Cant be helped. I'm going to write a comedy about it" (*Letters* 6:294). The "comedy" is almost certainly this story; the "damnable servility" is more problematic. Taken out of context, it would seem to indicate a dissatisfaction with her own marriage. This is certainly not the case. Virginia Woolf's marriage to Leonard is perhaps one of the happiest and most successful on record, in part because of the intimate games they invented to help keep it fresh and private. In these games, Virginia called herself "Mandril" (an African baboon), while Leonard was a mouse or mongoose. Dozens of their letters, even relatively late in their marriage (e.g., *Letters* 5:121, 123), attest to this. The term "damnable servility," therefore, unless written in a moment of pique, refers to Virginia's affection for and dependence on Leonard. She was in no sense a servile wife any more than he was a domineering husband.

All of this bears directly on a proper understanding of "Lappin and Lapinova." The story undeniably criticizes marriage, but marriage of a particular kind. Rosalind—the name evokes Shakespeare's independent heroine as well as Rosamond, Virginia Woolf's fictitious name for herself—is a bright, imaginative, and sensitive young woman. Her doubts about her marriage and the suitability of Ernest as a husband are present from the beginning. The name Ernest seems wrong to her, for it evokes images of "the Albert Memorial, mahogany sideboards, steel engravings of the Prince Consort with his family—her mother-in-law's dining room in Porchester Terrace in short" (255). The mention of Ernest's mother points to the heart of what she fears—that as part of the Thorburn family she will lose her identity and become nothing but a breeder of children and eventually a hard old "squire," the role she and Ernest assign old Mrs. Thorburn in their rabbit world. At the golden anniversary celebration she felt "a mere drop among all those Thorburns" (258) and, later at the dinner, "insoluble as an icicle" (258) that in the heat of the room "was being melted; dispersed; dissolved into nothingness" (259). The tension between Rosalind and her mother-in-law was mirrored in Virginia Woolf's relation to old Mrs. Woolf. Writing ten years before the story, she had said:

> Why did I hate it so? I felt the horror of family life, & the terrible threat to one's liberty that I used to feel with father, Aunt Mary, or George Duckworth. It is an emotion one never gets from any other human relationship. . . . But to be attached to her as a daughter would be so cruel a fate that I can think of nothing worse; & thousands of women might be dying of it in England today: this tyranny of mother over daughter, or father; their right to the due being as powerful as anything in the world. And then, they ask, why women dont write poetry. Short of killing Mrs. W. nothing could be done. Day after day one's life would be crumpled up like a bill for 10 pen[ce] 3 farthings. Nothing has ever been said of this. (*Diary* 3:194–95)

On this occasion, Rosalind is able to save herself by imagining the family in relation to the fantasy world of Lappin and Lapinova: her mother-in-law is the Squire, her sister-in-law Celia a ferret. More important, on the way home she and Ernest can laugh over the incident and share in the game.

The story's point, therefore, is not that marriage is necessarily bad for a woman, but that marriage to a young man like Ernest can be destructive. He resembles too closely the young men of "A Society" or "The Introduction," men who build office towers, conduct wars, and tear the wings from women who would fly free. Virginia Woolf's own marriage succeeded because the game of mandrill and mongoose outlasted the honeymoon—because, in short, she and Leonard maintained intimacy without surrendering identity.

"Lappin and Lapinova" is indeed among Virginia Woolf's finest stories in the conventional mode. The characters are alive, and the writing is sharp, clear, and pointed. The story line is well crafted and shrewdly paced, with a fine tension between moments of fear and periods of tenderness and fantasy. The world of rabbits and hares, which could easily seem silly or sentimental, is rendered with just the right tone of indulgence and seriousness so that it succeeds in conveying precisely the rhythm of the couple's relationship. Two years after the family party, for instance, when the vision can be called up only with some effort, we see perfectly what is happening: "It took him five minutes at least to change from Ernest Thorburn to King Lappin; and while she waited she felt a load on the back of her neck, as if somebody were about to wring it. At last he changed to King Lappin; his nose twitched; and they spent the evening roaming the woods much as usual" (260).

The imagery of the imaginary world of rabbits and hares runs throughout the story on both levels, the fanciful and the actual, uniting the two worlds and unifying the story's structural and emotional impact. The last sentence, "And that was the end of that marriage," comes like the blow Rosalind has been fearing, as swift and deadly as a poacher's cracking of a rabbit's neck.

The origin and evolution of "The Searchlight" has been traced in detail by J. W. Graham, who follows the story's progress from its beginnings in 1929 through its completion in 1941 and its publication in *A Haunted House* three years later. Graham locates the story's genesis in an episode Woolf read in *The Autobiography of Sir Henry Taylor* (1885), in which he reports looking through a telescope and seeing a couple kiss. Virginia Woolf worked and reworked her story around this incident, gradually adding a frame narrative and ordering events so that its theme becomes "the power of 'fiction' and language to absorb, preserve, transmute and transmit the *vital* reality of the past."[28] In this respect, the story harks back to "The Journal of Mistress Joan Martyn," whose theme and approach are similar in emphasizing the importance of ordinary events in history.

"The Searchlight" is narrated by a Mrs. Ivimey to a group of friends assembled on the balcony of an eighteenth-century mansion that now serves as a club. Searchlights are probing the London sky, practicing, for there is no war. One shaft of light falls in such a way as to remind Mrs. Ivimey of an incident in her great-grandfather's life, one so important that without it she would not be there to tell this story. She then relates how her great-grandfather, living in an isolated spot, turned his telescope one day on the landscape and spied a couple kissing passionately. He immediately ran from the house, found the girl, and married her, thus changing his life completely.

From these simple materials, Virginia Woolf creates a story of significant complex unity. The searchlights probing the London sky suggest war and the other large and "important" events that historians normally record, but they also are like the nighttime searching of the sky by the lonely young man in the tower on the moor. Randomly the searchlights illuminate now a portion of sky, now the blossoms on the chestnut trees, just as pure chance enabled the young man to see the couple kiss. This episode may be trivial from an historical perspective, but it is vital to Mrs. Ivimey's very existence, just as the fortunes of the Earl who constructed the house might in themselves seem insignificant, yet without them the present club would not exist. All of these apparently trivial details have been brought together in just the right combination to produce the story—a work of art that orders, illuminates, and liberates. In this brief and simple story, Virginia Woolf has succeeded completely where "The Journal of Mistress Joan Martyn" succeeded only partially. Both use a frame narrative; both express much the same idea, but "The Searchlight" is tightly constructed, economical, and unified in manner and message. To compare the two is to measure how far her art had progressed in the intervening years.

"Gipsy, the Mongrel" (1939; publ. 1985) is one of the most immediately appealing of Virginia Woolf's stories. Like "The Duchess and the Jeweller" and "The Shooting Party," it came about at the urging of Chambrun, the literary agent, who specifically asked for a dog story (*Diary* 5:241). Some months later, Woolf recorded that *Harper's Bazaar* had paid her £170 for the story (*Diary* 5:272), but for some reason it was not published in her lifetime. "Gipsy" is told in part by an omniscient narrator, who sets the scene and occasionally breaks in to comment or interpret, but most of it comes from the mouths of Tom and Lucy Bagot, who spin this "character study" (267) for their guests, the Bridgers. They describe Gipsy as a remarkable dog, half terrier and half something else, who three times escaped death by smiling in the face of it. She came to the Bagots and proved herself more a nuisance than a help in catching rats, but because of her charm and intelligence, the Bagots loved her. A well-meaning friend, thinking they should have a "real" dog, presented them with a handome red setter of impeccable pedigree, but it turned out to be polite, well-behaved, and stupid. Gipsy and Hector were opposites, but they got along well, until Hector began imitating Gipsy's bad behavior and had to be given away. Then one night, when London was as quiet as the country because of a snowfall, they heard a whistle. The next morning, Gipsy had disappeared.

No doubt the two dogs of this story, like the human characters in other fictions, are amalgams of many individuals Virginia Woolf knew. Three dogs mentioned in her letters and diaries, however, seem likely candidates for the original Gipsy. One was Tinker, a dog the Woolfs acquired in 1917. Tinker seems to have had a great deal of Gipsy's restless energy and curiosity, for Virginia Woolf several times describes him in her diary. On one occasion, "We have taken him for a walk, but directly he is loosed, he leaps walls, dashes into open doors, & behaves like a spirit in quest of something not to be found" (*Diary* 1:59–60). Like Gipsy, Tinker eventually ran off and was not found, even though his loss was reported to the police (*Diary* 1:72). Another model is Pinka (or Pinker), who came as a gift from Vita Sackville-West in 1929 and lived until 1935. One of Pinka's tricks was to put out Virginia Woolf's match, just as Gipsy would do for Lucy Bagot (*Diary* 4:317). The third was the mongrel Grizzle, mentioned by Virginia Woolf in a 1926 letter as being particularly affectionate, like most of its kind (*Letters* 3:253). Hector, the aristocratic thoroughbred of the story, is identifiable as Sally, an expensive purebred described as distinguished but of less solid character than Pinka and of questionable intelligence (*Diary* 4:328). The fact that Sally came right after Pinka in 1935 suggests that "Gipsy, The Mongrel" owes its genesis to the comparison of the two dogs.

Although "Gipsy, the Mongrel" is not great fiction, it is an excellent story for the popular press, certainly superior to most of its kind. For one thing, the manner of its telling is sophisticated and suggestive. The two couples are discussing a woman with a particularly appealing smile, when they hear a whistle or siren. That reminds the Bagots of Gipsy, and the story begins, but already Virginia Woolf has made an interesting observation, similar to that in "The Searchlight," about the strange way in which memory works by association.

As the tale progresses, Lucy Bagot frequently interrupts her husband's narrative to add comments or details, as does the omniscient author. These devices not only relieve the burden on Tom Bagot as narrator but also develop the Bagots as individuals. By the story's end, the tale of these two dogs has also shed significant light on their owners as people who recognize and appreciate true character. The details of Gipsy's life are amusing and interesting enough to carry the narrative swiftly along, and in the contrast between the lively, intelligent mongrel and the beautiful but foolish pedigree there is just enough parallel with humans to give the story a whiff of social commentary without allowing it to descend into cliché or mere fable. Finally, there is the autobiographical suggestion: as Virginia Woolf wrote to Ethel Smyth after the death of Pinka, a dog "represents . . . the private side of life—the play side" (*Letters* 5:396). This is a playful story with a touch of sentiment that reveals these aspects of its author's art and character.

"The Legacy" (1940; publ. 1944) returns to feminism in a manner reminiscent of "A Society" and "The Introduction." Like other stories of this period, it was written for *Harper's Bazaar* at the editor's request, but once again Woolf was disappointed by rejection. Even her angry letters, reminding the editor of their agreement, did no good, and she received no payment for the story (*Letters* 6:463, 469). The idea for the story itself can perhaps be traced, as Anne Oliver Bell suggests, to an incident shortly after the death of Lady Ottoline Morrell, when Woolf visited her husband Philip and was pressed by him to accept some of Ottoline's jewelry as a remembrance. She noted also at the time that Ottoline often confided in her maid Millie and that she put a great value on her diaries (*Diary* 5:140, 329–30). These details may have suggested a story in which a wife dies before her husband, leaving a distraught secretary and a neat shelf of diaries, from which the husband learns that she had fallen in love with another man and committed suicide a week after his death. The method of suicide used by Angela Clandon in the story may have been suggested by Milly Hamilton's remark years before that she wished she had the courage to step in front of a moving bus (*Diary* 2:167), or perhaps by the death of Virginia Woolf's Aunt Mary, who was run over by a car (*Diary* 2:114).

Why *Harper's Bazaar* rejected this story is a mystery, for it seems tailor made for a middlebrow audience. Gilbert Clandon, aged fifty, a minister in the current government, is insensitive and self-satisfied. His condescending attitude toward his wife's secretary, Sissy Miller, his indulgent amusement toward his wife's early diary entries, and his rising indignation as the diaries reveal her need for a lover mark him as pompous and complacent. The story's ending, in which Clandon learns that his wife committed suicide over the death of her lover, is too obviously ironic, and indeed the whole story seems contrived. Its characters are little more than stereotypes, and its theme is a cliché.

Happily, the last two stories, perhaps because they were not written for magazine publication, avoid these faults. "The Symbol" (1941; publ. 1985) records the thoughts of a woman on holiday in an Alpine village as she writes her sister in Birmingham and attempts to suggest what the mountain visible from her room symbolizes. Trying to avoid the usual clichés, she falls into reveries, recalling her long stay on the Isle of Wight, waiting impatiently for her mother to die. Descriptions of the Alpine village and its people, all of which strike her as slightly unreal, follow, until suddenly the climbers she had earlier mentioned disappear in a crevice.

This may not be great fiction, but it achieves freshness and originality by the paradoxical method of dealing with a hackneyed symbol. The letter writer's struggle to find an apt comparison for the mountain and her awareness of the usual trite similes lead to a series of associations that illuminate her character and the meaning of the mountain. The details she selects—the barrenness of the mountain top, the way it reminds her of the Isle of Wight, and the fact that it looms menacingly over the village—all suggest the mountain as a symbol of death. Equally important is the contrast between the "real" world outside the village and the "unreality" of the village and what happens in it. The two ideas are linked by the sudden disappearance of the climbers, who, she writes, "died in an attempt to discover" (284). The sentence is left unfinished. Much of the pleasure of this story lies in the challenge of finding meaning where the letter writer cannot and in savoring Woolf's precise but evocative prose. It is difficult to accept, however, that the woman could have seen the climbers disappear, but this is the only false note in an otherwise artful story.

"The Watering Place" (1941; publ. 1985) is the kind of short sketch that was popular in the 1920s and 1930s among writers influenced by Chekhov. In this type of story, there is no plot line but only a series of incidents that by their arrangement and emphasis suggest a pattern. This one opens with a description of a seaside village and its people, comparing them to shells, "as if the real animal had been extracted on the point of a pin and only the shell remained" (285). The story then cuts, in the cinematic sense, to a ladies' room in a restaurant, where three young working-class women are tidying their makeup and talking. Their fragmentary chatter about men is similar to the conversation between the two women in "Kew Gardens"—shallow and trite. A toilet flushes and the scene ends, followed by a brief description of the town at night, comparing it to a skeleton picked out in lights.

Few of Woolf's stories are as bitter as this one or as literal a transcription of an actual experience. The experience occurred at Brighton in February of 1941, and the diary entry is largely a record of the dialogue she overheard in the ladies' room of the Sussex Grill. Her comment on it is instructive: "They were powdering & painting, these common little tarts, while I sat, behind a thin door, p——ing as quietly as I could" (*Diary* 5:356–57). Since Virginia Woolf's suicide followed this event by just over a month, we may conclude that her disgust at these "tarts" was part of her general depression at the time. Considering that England was then plunged into the worst war in its history, fighting for its survival, her irritation at these women is understandable. The story is not accomplished or profound, but it is strangely optimistic in that it represents yet one more attempt to master the form that many consider the most difficult in prose.

Virginia Woolf's last piece of fiction, like her first, grew out of personal experience and reflected her state of mind at the time. Since that first story, she had explored the form over a period of more than forty years, incorporating her ideas and experiences into some forty-five pieces of short fiction. As we have seen, the impetus for these stories often derived from incidents in her personal life—anxieties over her role as a woman, persons she had met and observed, situations she encountered at parties, even dogs she had owned and snatches of conversation she overheard. One cannot trace in Virginia Woolf's short fiction the important patterns and movements in her life as one can detect the pain she felt over her brother Thoby's loss in *Jacob's Room* or the essential features of her family life in *To the Lighthouse*. Nevertheless, the connection between biography and art is fascinating and illuminating. More important than the biographic details are the thematic concerns of the stories, for these reflect inevitably Virginia Woolf's thinking. Of these, feminist issues are among the most important and enduring, being visible in the earliest story, "Phyllis and Rosamond," and in one of the last, "The Legacy." Related to this is the unequal struggle, as she saw it, in the battle between the sexes, one that happily did not affect her married life with Leonard. Likewise, she was concerned about knowledge—how we acquire and validate it, and what uses we find for it. Her radically different view of history, in which social history counts for more than political and military pageantry, is related to her feminism and her sense of what is important in life. Her distrust of externals and her passionate belief in the importance of the inner life led her to seek new ways of apprehending and presenting character. To achieve this, she pioneered advances in literary psychology as well as new devices in style and technique. Recognizing the subjectivity of experience and the importance of point of view (in both the literary and the philosophical senses) enabled her to depict the difficulties of communication that have become one of the century's chief literary concerns.

Virginia Woolf's reputation will always rest primarily on her novels, but she left behind a body of short fiction that will stand favorable comparison with stories of the best of her contemporaries. Her contribution is often thought to be in the lyrical story only, but as this survey has suggested, she excelled in stories of many types, including the conventional. Although she wrote little about the theory behind her short fiction, we can infer from her restless experimentation and constant revision that she strove for formal perfection and psychological understanding in her short fiction as well as in her novels. She succeeded in her aim more often than most and left behind a collected short fiction of great richness and variety.

We are just beginning to appreciate her achievement.

Notes

1. Jean Guiguet, *Virginia Woolf and Her Works*, trans. Jean Stewart (London: Hogarth Press, 1965), 329–43.

2. Susan Dick, ed., *The Complete Shorter Fiction of Virginia Woolf* (New York: Harcourt, Brace, Jovanovich, 1985). All quotations from the stories will be taken from this collection and cited in the text.

3. Stella McNichol, ed., *Mrs. Dalloway's Party: A Short Story Sequence* (London: Hogarth Press, 1973; New York: Harcourt, Brace, Jovanovich, 1975).

4. *The Diary of Virginia Woolf*, ed. Anne Olivier Bell, 5 vols. (New York: Harcourt, Brace, Jovanovich, 1977–84), 3:87. Hereafter references to the *Diary* will be cited in the text by volume and page.

5. Louise A. DeSalvo, "Shakespeare's *Other* Sister," in *New Feminist Essays on Virginia Woolf*, ed. Jane Marcus (Lincoln: University of Nebraska Press), 61–81.

6. Anthony Alpers, *The Life of Katherine Mansfield* (New York: Viking Press, 1980), 251–52.

7. Avrom Fleishman, "Forms of the Woolfian Short Story," in *Virginia Woolf: Revaluation and Continuity*, ed. Ralph Freedman (Berkeley: University of California Press, 1980), 44–70.

8. *The Letters of Virginia Woolf*, ed. Nigel Nicolson and Joanne Trautmann, 6 vols. (New York: Harcourt, Brace, Jovanovich, 1975–80), 2:299. Hereafter references to the *Letters* will be cited in the text by volume and page.

9. Robert A. Watson, "'Solid Objects' as Allegory," *Virginia Woolf Miscellany* 16 (1980):3–4.

10. Virginia Hastings Floyd, "The Unspoken Word," in *Studies in Interpretation*, ed. Esther M. Doyle (Amsterdam: Rodopi NV, 1972), 191–203.

11. Lyndall Gordon, *Virginia Woolf: A Writer's Life* (New York: W. W. Norton, 1984), 170.

12. Stephen D. Fox, " 'An Unwritten Novel' and a Hidden Protagonist," *Virginia Woolf Quarterly* 4 (1973):70, 75.

13. Quentin Bell, *Virginia Woolf: A Biography*, 2 vols. (New York: Harcourt, Brace, Jovanovich, 1972), 1:157–61, 213–16.

14. Susan Dick, "'What fools we were!': Virginia Woolf's 'A Society,'" *Twentieth Century Literature* 33 (Spring 1987):51–66.

15. *Collected Essays*, ed. Leonard Woolf, 4 vols. (London: Hogarth Press, 1966). 1:336. Hereafter cited in the text as *Essays*.

16. Charles G. Hoffmann, "From Short Story to Novel: The Manuscript Revisions of Virginia Woolf's *Mrs. Dalloway*," *Modern Fiction Studies* 14 (Summer 1968):171–86.

17. Judith P. Saunders, "Moral Stain: Literary Allusion and Female Sexuality in 'Mrs. Dalloway in Bond Street,'" *Studies in Short Fiction* 15 (Spring 1978):144.

18. Bell, *Woolf*, 2:95, 110.

19. Gordon, *Writer's Life*, 28–39.

20. Ibid., 12–15.

21. Cf. Phyllis Rose, *Woman of Letters: A Life of Virginia Woolf* (New York: Oxford University Press, 1978), 94–97.

22. Joanne Trautmann Banks, "Virginia Woolf and Katherine Mansfield," in *The English Short Story 1880–1945*, ed. Joseph M. Flora (Boston: Twayne, 1985), 60.

23. Ibid., 60.

24. Virginia Woolf, *To the Lighthouse* (New York: Harcourt, Brace, & World, 1955), 292.

25. Gordon, *Writer's Life*, 158–59.

26. Bell, *Woolf*, 2:81–83.

27. Gordon, *Writer's Life*, 141–146.

28. J. W. Graham, "The Drafts of Virginia Woolf's 'The Searchlight,'" *Twentieth Century Literature* 12 (1976):390.

Part 2

THE WRITER

Introduction

Virginia Woolf's two famous essays, "Mr. Bennett and Mrs. Brown" and "Modern Fiction," together constitute her personal fictional credo and one of the clearest and most forceful apologias for the modernist movement. Like most such writings, they are in effect a defense of the writer's own practices and aesthetic and in this respect can be compared to Wordsworth's preface to the *Lyrical Ballads*, T. S. Eliot's "Tradition and Individual Talent," or F. S. Flynt's essays on imagism.

Both essays argue much the same point, that Edwardian fiction as represented by Arnold Bennett, H. G. Wells, and John Galsworthy is no longer capable of doing what fiction must do—elucidate character. That is because, Virginia Woolf says (at least partly tongue in cheek), human nature changed in December 1910. "Mr. Bennett and Mrs. Brown" illustrates its thesis by presenting Mrs. Brown and then imagining how each of the aforementioned novelists would attempt in vain to capture her personality. The similarity between Woolf's example in the essay and her methods in such stories as "An Unwritten Novel," "Moments of Being: Slater's Pins Have No Points," "The Lady in the Looking Glass: A Reflection," and "The Shooting Party" is obvious.

"Modern Fiction" argues that the Edwardian novelists are "materialists," concentrating on the surfaces of life, missing its essence and spirit. Its justly famous passage describing life as a "luminous halo" explains the psychological theory at work in Woolf's novels and stories. The discussion of Chekhov's "Gusev" as an example of the modernist method suggests that she was not confining her remarks to the novel alone.

As noted in the preceding essay, Woolf's theory and method slowly moved away from the principals outlined in these essays toward more traditional techniques. Unfortunately, no similar manifesto exists in her critical writings, letters, or diaries to explain the shift evident both in the novels and stories. What is missing, however, matters less in this case than what exists, for what we have in Virginia Woolf's essays in general and these two in particular are powerful, insightful, and witty statements of what she and her contemporaries hoped to achieve—and often did—in their most memorable work.

Mr. Bennett and Mrs. Brown*

It seems to me possible, perhaps desirable, that I may be the only person in this room who has committed the folly of writing, trying to write, or failing to write, a novel. And when I asked myself, as your invitation to speak to you about modern fiction made me ask myself, what demon whispered in my eàr and urged me to my doom, a little figure rose before me—the figure of a man, or of a woman, who said, "My name is Brown. Catch me if you can."

Most novelists have the same experience. Some Brown, Smith, or Jones comes before them and says in the most seductive and charming way in the world, "Come and catch me if you can." And so, led on by this will-o'-the-wisp, they flounder through volume after volume, spending the best years of their lives in the pursuit, and receiving for the most part very little cash in exchange. Few catch the phantom; most have to be content with a scrap of her dress or a wisp of her hair.

My belief that men and women write novels because they are lured on to create some character which has thus imposed itself upon them has the sanction of Mr. Arnold Bennett. In an article from which I will quote he says, "The foundation of good fiction is character-creating and nothing else. . . . Style counts; plot counts; originality of outlook counts. But none of these counts anything like so much as the convincingness of the characters. If the characters are real the novel will have a chance; if they are not, oblivion will be its portion. . . . "And he goes on to draw the conclusion that we have no young novelists of first-rate importance at the present moment, because they are unable to create characters that are real, true, and convincing.

These are the questions that I want with greater boldness than discretion to discuss tonight. I want to make out what we mean when we talk about "character" in fiction; to say something about the question

*This essay was originally a paper read to the Heretics, Cambridge, 18 May 1924.
From *The Captain's Death Bed and Other Essays* by Virginia Woolf (New York: Harcourt Brace Jovanovich, 1950). Copyright 1950, 1978 by Harcourt Brace Jovanovich, Inc. Reprinted by permission of the publisher.

of reality which Mr. Bennett raises; and to suggest some reasons why the younger novelists fail to create characters, if, as Mr. Bennett asserts, it is true that fail they do. This will lead me, I am well aware, to make some very sweeping and some very vague assertions. For the question is an extremely difficult one. Think how little we know about character—think how little we know about art. But, to make a clearance before I begin, I will suggest that we range Edwardians and Georgians into two camps; Mr. Wells, Mr. Bennett, and Mr. Galsworthy I will call the Edwardians; Mr. Forster, Mr. Lawrence, Mr. Strachey, Mr. Joyce, and Mr. Eliot I will call the Georgians. And if I speak in the first person, with intolerable egotism, I will ask you to excuse me. I do not want to attribute to the world at large the opinions of one solitary, ill-informed, and misguided individual.

My first assertion is one that I think you will grant—that everyone in this room is a judge of character. Indeed it would be impossible to live for a year without disaster unless one practised character-reading and had some skill in the art. Our marriages, our friendships depend on it; our business largely depends on it; every day questions arise which can only be solved by its help. And now I will hazard a second assertion, which is more disputable perhaps, to the effect that in or about December, 1910, human character changed.

I am not saying that one went out, as one might into a garden, and there saw that a rose had flowered, or that a hen had laid an egg. The change was not sudden and definite like that. But a change there was, nevertheless; and, since one must be arbitrary, let us date it about the year 1910. The first signs of it are recorded in the books of Samuel Butler, in *The Way of All Flesh* in particular; the plays of Bernard Shaw continue to record it. In life one can see the change, if I may use a homely illustration, in the character of one's cook. The Victorian cook lived like a leviathan in the lower depths, formidable, silent, obscure, inscrutable; the Georgian cook is a creature of sunshine and fresh air; in and out of the drawing-room, now to borrow the *Daily Herald*, now to ask advice about a hat. Do you ask for more solemn instances of the power of the human race to change? Read the *Agamemnon*, and see whether, in process of time, your sympathies are not almost entirely with Clytemnestra. Or consider the married life of the Carlyles and bewail the waste, the futility, for him and for her, of the horrible domestic tradition which made it seemly for a woman of genius to spend her time chasing beetles, scouring saucepans, instead of writing books. All human relations have shifted—those between masters and servants,

Mr. Bennett and Mrs. Brown

husbands and wives, parents and children. And when human relations
change there is at the same time a change in religion, conduct, politics,
and literature. Let us agree to place one of these changes about the
year 1910.

I have said that people have to acquire a good deal of skill in character-reading if they are to live a single year of life without disaster.
But it is the art of the young. In middle age and in old age the art is
practised mostly for its uses, and friendships and other adventures and
experiments in the art of reading character are seldom made. But novelists differ from the rest of the world because they do not cease to be
interested in character when they have learnt enough about it for practical purposes. They go a step further, they feel that there is something
permanently interesting in character in itself. When all the practical
business of life has been discharged, there is something about people
which continues to seem to them of overwhelming importance, in spite
of the fact that it has no bearing whatever upon their happiness, comfort, or income. The study of character becomes to them an absorbing
pursuit; to impart character an obsession. And this I find it very difficult to explain: what novelists mean when they talk about character,
what the impulse is that urges them so powerfully every now and then
to embody their view in writing.

So if you will allow me, instead of analysing and abstracting, I will
tell you a simple story which, however pointless, has the merit of being
true, of a journey from Richmond to Waterloo, in the hope that I may
show you what I mean by character in itself; that you may realize the
different aspects it can wear; and the hideous perils that beset you
directly you try to describe it in words.

One night some weeks ago, then, I was late for the train and jumped
into the first carriage I came to. As I sat down I had the strange and
uncomfortable feeling that I was interrupting a conversation between
two people who were already sitting there. Not that they were young
or happy. Far from it. They were both elderly, the woman over sixty,
the man well over forty. They were sitting opposite each other, and
the man, who had been leaning over and talking emphatically to judge
by his attitude and the flush on his face, sat back and became silent. I
had disturbed him, and he was annoyed. The elderly lady, however,
whom I will call Mrs. Brown, seemed rather relieved. She was one of
those clean, threadbare old ladies whose extreme tidiness—everything
buttoned, fastened, tied together, mended and brushed up—suggests
more extreme poverty than rags and dirt. There was something

81

pinched about her—a look of suffering, of apprehension, and, in addition, she was extremely small. Her feet, in their clean little boots, scarcely touched the floor. I felt she had nobody to support her; that she had to make up her mind for herself; that, having been deserted, or left a widow, years ago, she had led an anxious, harried life, bringing up an only son, perhaps, who, as likely as not, was by this time beginning to go to the bad. All this shot through my mind as I sat down, being uncomfortable, like most people, at travelling with fellow passengers unless I have somehow or other accounted for them. Then I looked at the man. He was no relation of Mrs. Brown's I felt sure; he was of a bigger, burlier, less refined type. He was a man of business I imagined, very likely a respectable corn-chandler from the North, dressed in good blue serge with a pocket-knife and a silk handerchief, and a stout leather bag. Obviously, however, he had an unpleasant business to settle with Mrs. Brown; a secret, perhaps sinister business, which they did not intend to discuss in my presence.

"Yes, the Crofts have had very bad luck with their servants," Mr. Smith (as I will call him) said in a considering way, going back to some earlier topic, with a view to keeping up appearances.

"Ah, poor people," said Mrs. Brown, a trifle condescendingly. "My grandmother had a maid who came when she was fifteen and stayed till she was eighty" (this was said with a kind of hurt and aggressive pride to impress us both perhaps).

"One doesn't often come across that sort of thing nowadays," said Mr. Smith in conciliatory tones.

Then they were silent.

"It's odd they don't start a golf club there—I should have thought one of the young fellows would," said Mr. Smith, for the silence obviously made him uneasy.

Mrs. Brown hardly took the trouble to answer.

"What changes they're making in this part of the world," said Mr. Smith looking out of the window, and looking furtively at me as he did so.

It was plain, from Mrs. Brown's silence, from the uneasy affability with which Mr. Smith spoke, that he had some power over her which he was exerting disagreeably. It might have been her son's downfall, or some painful episode in her past life, or her daughter's. Perhaps she was going to London to sign some document to make over some property. Obviously against her will she was in Mr. Smith's hands. I was

Mr. Bennett and Mrs. Brown

beginning to feel a great deal of pity for her, when she said, suddenly and inconsequently:

"Can you tell me if an oak-tree dies when the leaves have been eaten for two years in succession by caterpillars?"

She spoke quite brightly, and rather precisely, in a cultivated, inquisitive voice.

Mr. Smith was startled, but relieved to have a safe topic of conversation given him. He told her a great deal very quickly about plagues of insects. He told her that he had a brother who kept a fruit farm in Kent. He told her what fruit farmers do every year in Kent, and so on, and so on. While he talked a very odd thing happened. Mrs. Brown took out her little white handkerchief and began to dab her eyes. She was crying. But she went on listening quite composedly to what he was saying, and he went on talking, a little louder, a little angrily, as if he had seen her cry often before; as if it were a painful habit. At last it got on his nerves. He stopped abruptly, looked out of the window, then leant towards her as he had been doing when I got in, and said in a bullying, menacing way, as if he would not stand any more nonsense: "So about the matter we were discussing. It'll be all right? George will be there on Tuesday?"

"We shan't be late," said Mrs. Brown, gathering herself together with superb dignity.

Mr. Smith said nothing. He got up, buttoned his coat, reached his bag down, and jumped out of the train before it had stopped at Clapham Junction. He had got what he wanted, but he was ashamed of himself; he was glad to get out of the old lady's sight.

Mrs. Brown and I were left alone together. She sat in her corner opposite, very clean, very small, rather queer, and suffering intensely. The impression she made was overwhelming. It came pouring out like a draught, like a smell of burning. What was it composed of—that overwhelming and peculiar impression? Myriads of irrelevant and incongruous ideas crowed into one's head on such occasions; one sees the person, one sees Mrs. Brown, in the centre of all sorts of different scenes. I thought of her in a seaside house, among queer ornaments: sea-urchins, models of ships in glass cases. Her husband's medals were on the mantelpiece. She popped in and out of the room, perching on the edges of chairs, picking meals out of saucers, indulging in long, silent stares. The caterpillars and the oak-trees seemed to imply all that. And then, into this fantastic and secluded life, in broke Mr.

Smith. I saw him blowing in, so to speak, on a windy day. He banged, he slammed. His dripping umbrella made a pool in the hall. They sat closeted together.

And then Mrs. Brown faced the dreadful revelation. She took her heroic decision. Early, before dawn, she packed her bag and carried it herself to the station. She would not let Smith touch it. She was wounded in her pride, unmoored from her anchorage; she came of gentlefolks who kept servants—but details could wait. The important thing was to realize her character, to steep oneself in her atmosphere. I had no time to explain why I felt it somewhat tragic, heroic, yet with a dash of the flighty, and fantastic, before the train stopped, and I watched her disappear, carrying her bag, into the vast blazing station. She looked very small, very tenacious; at once very frail and very heroic. And I have never seen her again, and I shall never know what became of her.

The story ends without any point to it. But I have not told you this anecdote to illustrate either my own ingenuity or the pleasure of travelling from Richmond to Waterloo. What I want you to see in it is this. Here is a character imposing itself upon another person. Here is Mrs. Brown making someone begin almost automatically to write a novel about her. I believe that all novels begin with an old lady in the corner opposite. I believe that all novels, that is to say, deal with character, and that it is to express character—not to preach doctrines, sing songs, or celebrate the glories of the British Empire, that the form of the novel, so clumsy, verbose, and undramatic, so rich, elastic, and alive, has been evolved. To express character, I have said; but you will at once reflect that the very widest interpretation can be put upon those words. For example, old Mrs. Brown's character will strike you very differently according to the age and country in which you happen to be born. It would be easy enough to write three different versions of that incident in the train, an English, a French, and a Russian. The English writer would make the old lady into a "character"; he would bring out her oddities and mannerisms; her buttons and wrinkles; her ribbons and warts. Her personality would dominate the book. A French writer would rub out all that; he would sacrifice the individual Mrs. Brown to give a more general view of human nature; to make a more abstract, proportioned, and harmonious whole. The Russian would pierce through the flesh; would reveal the soul—the soul alone, wandering out into the Waterloo Road, asking of life some tremendous question which would sound on and on in our ears after the book was finished. And then besides age and country there is the writer's temperament to be considered. You see one thing in character, and I another. You say it means this, and I that. And when it comes to writing, each makes a further selection on principles of his own. Thus Mrs. Brown can be treated in an infinite variety of ways, according to the age, country, and temperament of the writer.

But now I must recall what Mr. Arnold Bennett says. He says that it is only if the characters are real that the novel has any chance of surviving. Otherwise, die it must. But, I ask myself, what is reality? And who are the judges of reality? A character may be real to Mr. Bennett and quite unreal to me. For instance, in this article he says that Dr. Watson in *Sherlock Holmes* is real to him: to me Dr. Watson is a sack stuffed with straw, a dummy, a figure of fun. And so it is with character after character—in book after book. There is nothing that people differ about more than the reality of characters, especially in contemporary books. But if you take a larger view I think that Mr. Bennett is perfectly right. If, that is, you think of the novels which seem to you great novels—*War and Peace, Vanity Fair, Tristram Shandy, Madame Bovary, Pride and Prejudice, The Mayor of Casterbridge, Villette*—if you think of these books, you do at once think of some character who seemed to you so real (I do not by that mean so lifelike) that it has the power to make you think not merely of it itself, but of all sorts of things through its eyes—of religion, of love, of war, of peace, of family life, of balls in country towns, of sunsets, moonrises, the immortality of the soul. There is hardly any subject of human experience that is left out of *War and Peace* it seems to me. And in all these novels all these great novelists have brought us to see whatever they wish us to see through some character. Otherwise, they would not be novelists; but poets, historians, or pamphleteers.

But now let us examine what Mr. Bennett went on to say—he said that there was no great novelist among the Georgian writers because they cannot create characters who are real, true, and convincing. And there I cannot agree. There are reasons, excuses, possibilities which I think put a different colour upon the case. It seems so to me at least, but I am well aware that this is a matter about which I am likely to be prejudiced, sanguine, and near-sighted. I will put my view before you in the hope that you will make it impartial, judicial, and broad-minded. Why, then, is it so hard for novelists at present to create characters which seem real, not only to Mr. Bennett, but to the world at large? Why, when October comes round, do the publishers always fail to supply us with a masterpiece?

Surely one reason is that the men and women who began writing novels in 1910 or thereabouts had this great difficulty to face—that there was no English novelist living from whom they could learn their business. Mr. Conrad is a Pole; which sets him apart, and makes him, however admirable, not very helpful. Mr. Hardy has written no novel since 1895. The most prominent and successful novelists in the year 1910 were, I suppose, Mr. Wells, Mr. Bennett, and Mr. Galsworthy. Now it seems to me that to go to these men and ask them to teach you how to write a novel—how to create characters that are real—is precisely like going to a bootmaker and asking him to teach you how to make a watch. Do not let me give you the impression that I do not admire and enjoy their books. They seem to me of great value, and indeed of great necessity. There are seasons when it is more important to have boots than to have watches. To drop metaphor, I think that after the creative activity of the Victorian age it was quite necessary, not only for literature but for life, that someone should write the books that Mr. Wells, Mr. Bennett, and Mr. Galsworthy have written. Yet what odd books they are! Sometimes I wonder if we are right to call them books at all. For they leave one with so strange a feeling of incompleteness and dissatisfaction. In order to complete them it seems necessary to do something—to join a society, or, more desperately, to write a cheque. That done, the restlessness is laid, the book finished; it can be put upon the shelf, and need never be read again. But with the work of other novelists it is different. *Tristram Shandy* or *Pride and Prejudice* is complete in itself; it is self-contained; it leaves one with no desire to do anything, except indeed to read the book again, and to understand it better. The difference perhaps is that both Sterne and Jane Austen were interested in things in themselves; in character in itself; in the book in itself. Therefore everything was inside the book, nothing outside. But the Edwardians were never interested in character in itself; or in the book in itself. They were interested in something outside. Their books, then, were incomplete as books, and required that the reader should finish them, actively and practically, for himself.

Perhaps we can make this clearer if we take the liberty of imagining a little party in the railway carriage—Mr. Wells, Mr. Galsworthy, Mr. Bennett are travelling to Waterloo with Mrs. Brown. Mrs. Brown, I have said, was poorly dressed and very small. She had an anxious, harassed look. I doubt whether she was what you call an educated woman. Seizing upon all these symptoms of the unsatisfactory condition of our primary schools with a rapidity to which I can do no justice, Mr. Wells would intantly project upon the window-pane a vision of a better, breezier, jollier, happier, more adventurous and gallant world, where these musty railway carriages and fusty old women do not exist; where miraculous barges bring tropical fruit to Camberwell by eight o'clock in the morning; where there are public nurseries, fountains, and libraries, dining-rooms, drawing-rooms, and marriages; where every citizen is generous and candid, manly and magnificent, and rather like Mr. Wells himself. But nobody is in the least like Mrs. Brown. There are no Mrs. Browns in Utopia. Indeed I do not think that Mr. Wells, in his passion to make her what she ought to be, would waste a thought upon her as she is. And what would Mr. Galsworthy see? Can we doubt that the walls of Doulton's factory would take his fancy? There are women in that factory who make twenty-five dozen earthenware pots every day. There are mothers in the Mile End Road who depend upon the farthings which those women earn. But there are employers in Surrey who are even now smoking rich cigars while the nightingale sings. Burning with indignation, stuffed with information, arraigning civilization, Mr. Galsworthy would only see in Mrs. Brown a pot broken on the wheel and thrown into the corner.

Mr. Bennett, alone of the Edwardians, would keep his eyes in the carriage. He, indeed, would observe every detail with immense care. He would notice the advertisements; the pictures of Swanage and Portsmouth; the way in which the cushion bulged between the buttons; how Mrs. Brown wore a brooch which had cost three-and-ten-three at Whitworth's bazaar; and had mended both gloves—indeed the thumb of the left-hand glove had been replaced. And he would observe, at length, how this was the non-stop train from Windsor which calls at Richmond for the convenience of middle-class residents, who can afford to go to the theatre but have not reached the social rank which can afford motor-cars, though it is true, there are occasions (he would tell us what), when they hire them from a company (he would tell us which). And so he would gradually sidle sedately towards Mrs. Brown, and would remark how she had been left a little copyhold, not freehold, property at Datchet, which, however, was mortgaged to Mr. Bungay the solicitor—but why should I presume to invent Mr. Bennett? Does not Mr. Bennett write novels himself? I will open the first book that chance puts in my way—*Hilda Lessways*. Let us see how he makes us feel that Hilda is real, true, and convincing, as a novelist should. She shut the door in a soft, controlled way, which showed the constraint of her relations with her mother. She was fond of reading *Maud*; she was endowed with the power to feel intensely. So far, so good; in his leisurely, surefooted way Mr. Bennett is trying in these first pages, where every touch is important, to show us the kind of girl she was.

But then he begins to describe, not Hilda Lessways, but the view from her bedroom window, the excuse being that Mr. Skellorn, the man who collects rents, is coming along that way. Mr. Bennett proceeds:

"The bailiwick of Turnhill lay behind her; and all the murky district of the Five Towns, of which Turnhill is the northern outpost, lay to the south. At the foot of Chatterley Wood the canal wound in large curves on its way towards the undefiled plains of Cheshire and the sea. On the canal-side, exactly opposite to Hilda's window, was a flour-mill, that sometimes made nearly as much smoke as the kilns and the chimneys closing the prospect on either hand. From the flour-mill a bricked path, which separated a considerable row of new cottages from their appurtenant gardens, led straight into Lessways Street, in front of Mrs. Lessways' house. By this path Mr. Skellorn should have arrived, for he inhabited the farthest of the cottages."

One line of insight would have done more than all those lines of description; but let them pass as the necessary drudgery of the novelist. And now—where is Hilda? Alas. Hilda is still looking out of the window. Passionate and dissatisfied as she was, she was a girl with an eye for houses. She often compared this old Mr. Skellorn with the villas she saw from her bedroom window. Therefore the villas must be described. Mr. Bennett proceeds:

"The row was called Freehold Villas: a consciously proud name in a district where much of the land was copyhold and could only change owners subject to the payment of 'fines,' and to the feudal consent of a 'court' presided over by the agent of a lord of the manor. Most of the dwellings were owned by their occupiers, who, each an absolute monarch of the soil, niggled in his sooty garden of an evening amid the flutter of drying shirts and towels. Freehold Villas symbolized the final triumph of Victorian economics, the apotheosis of the prudent and industrious artisan. It corresponded with a Building Society Secretary's dream of paradise. And indeed it was a very real achievement. Nevertheless, Hilda's irrational contempt would not admit this."

Heaven be praised, we cry! At last we are coming to Hilda herself. But not so fast. Hilda may have been this, that, and the other; but Hilda not only looked at houses, and thought of houses; Hilda lived in a house. And what sort of a house did Hilda live in? Mr. Bennett proceeds:

"It was one of the two middle houses of a detached terrace of four houses built by her grandfather Lessways, the teapot manufacturer; it was the chief of the four, obviously the habitation of the proprietor of the terrace. One of the corner houses comprised a grocer's shop, and this house had been robbed of its just proportion of garden so that the seigneurial garden-plot might be triflingly larger than the other. The terrace was not a terrace of cottages, but of houses rated at from twenty-six to thirty-six pounds a year; beyond the means of artisans and petty insurance agents and rent-collectors. And further, it was well-built, generously built; and its architecture, though debased, showed some faint traces of Georgian amenity. It was admittedly the best row of houses in that newly-settled quarter of the town. In coming to it out of Freehold Villas Mr. Skellorn obviously came to something superior, wider, more liberal. Suddenly Hilda heard her mother's voice. . . ."

But we cannot hear her mother's voice, or Hilda's voice; we can only hear Mr. Bennett's voice telling us facts about rents and freeholds and copyholds and fines. What can Mr. Bennett be about? I have formed my own opinion of what Mr. Bennett is about—he is trying to make us imagine for him; he is trying to hypnotize us into the belief that, because he has made a house, there must be a person living there. With all his powers of observation, which are marvellous, with all his sympathy and humanity, which are great, Mr. Bennett has never once looked at Mrs. Brown in her corner. There she sits in the corner of the carriage—that carriage which is travelling, not from Richmond to Waterloo, but from one age of English literature to the next, for Mrs. Brown is eternal, Mrs. Brown is human nature, Mrs. Brown changes only on the surface, it is the novelists who get in and out—there she sits and not one of the Edwardian writers has so much as looked at her. They have looked very powerfully, searchingly, and sympathetically out of the window; at factories, at Utopias, even at the decoration and upholstery of the carriage; but never at her, never at life, never at human nature. And so they have developed a technique of novel-writing which suits their purpose; they have made tools and established conventions which do their business. But those tools are not our tools, and that business is not our business. For us those conventions are ruin, those tools are death.

You may well complain of the vagueness of my language. What is a convention, a tool, you may ask, and what do you mean by saying that Mr. Bennett's and Mr. Wells's and Mr. Galsworthy's conventions are the wrong conventions for the Georgians? The question is difficult: I will attempt a short-cut. A convention in writing is not much different from a convention in manners. Both in life and in literature it is necessary to have some means of bridging the gulf between the hostess and her unknown guest on the one hand, the writer and his unknown reader on the other. The hostess bethinks her of the weather, for generations of hostesses have established the fact that this is a subject of universal interest in which we all believe. She begins by saying that we are having a wretched May, and, having thus got into touch with her unknown guest, proceeds to matters of greater interest. So it is in literature. The writer must get into touch with his reader by putting before him something which he recognizes, which therefore stimulates his imagination, and makes him willing to cooperate in the far more difficult business of intimacy. And it is of the highest importance that this common meeting-place should be reached easily, amost instinctively, in the dark, with one's eyes shut. Here is Mr. Bennett making use of this common ground in the passage which I have quoted. The problem before him was to make us believe in the reality of Hilda Lessways. So he began, being an Edwardian, by describing accurately and minutely the sort of house Hilda lived in, and the sort of house she saw from the window. House property was the common ground from which the Edwardians found it easy to proceed to intimacy. Indirect as it seems to us, the convention worked admirably, and thousands of Hilda Lessways were launched upon the world by this means. For that age and generation, the convention was a good one.

But now, if you will allow me to pull my own anecdote to pieces, you will see how keenly I felt the lack of a convention, and how serious a matter it is when the tools of one generation are useless for the next. The incident had made a great impression on me. But how was I to transmit it to you? All I could do was to report as accurately as I could what was said, to describe in detail what was worn, to say, despairingly, that all sorts of scenes rushed into my mind, to procced to tumble them out pell-mell, and to describe this vivid, this overmastering impression by likening it to a draught or a smell of burning. To tell you the truth, I was also strongly tempted to manufacture a three-volume novel about the old lady's son, and his adventures crossing the Atlantic, and her daughter, and how she kept a milliner's shop in Westminster, the past life of Smith himself, and his house at Sheffield, though such stories seem to me the most dreary, irrelevant, and humbugging affairs in the world.

But if I had done that I should have escaped the appalling effort of saying what I meant. And to have got at what I meant I should have had to go back and back; to experiment with one thing and another; to try this sentence and that, referring each word to my vision, matching it as exactly as possible, and knowing that somehow I had to find a common ground between us, a convention which would not seem to you too odd, unreal, and farfetched to believe in. I admit that I shirked that arduous undertaking. I let my Mrs. Brown slip through my fingers. I have told you nothing whatever about her. But that is partly the great Edwardians' fault. I asked them—they are my elders and betters— How shall I begin to describe this woman's character? And they said: "Begin by saying that her father kept a shop in Harrogate. Ascertain the rent. Ascertain the wages of shop assistants in the year 1878. Discover what her mother died of. Describe cancer. Describe calico. Describe————" But I cried: "Stop! Stop!" And I regret to say that I threw that ugly, that clumsy, that incongruous tool out of the window, for I knew that if I began describing the cancer and the calico, my Mrs. Brown, that vision to which I cling though I know no way of imparting it to you, would have been dulled and tarnished and vanished for ever.

That is what I mean by saying that the Edwardian tools are the wrong ones for us to use. They have laid an enormous stress upon the fabric of things. They have given us a house in the hope that we may be able to deduce the human beings who live there. To give them their due, they have made that house much better worth living in. But if you hold that novels are in the first place about people, and only in the second about the houses they live in, that is the wrong way to set about it. Therefore, you see, the Georgian writer had to begin by throwing away the method that was in use at the moment. He was left alone there facing Mrs. Brown without any method of conveying her to the reader. But that is inaccurate. A writer is never alone. There is always the public with him—if not on the same seat, at least in the compartment next door. Now the public is a strange travelling companion. In England it is a very suggestive and docile creature, which, once you get it to attend, will believe implicitly what it is told for a certain number of years. If you say to the public with sufficient conviction: "All women have tails, and all men humps," it will actually learn to see women with tails and men with humps, and will think it very revolutionary and probably improper if you say: "Nonsense. Monkeys have tails and camels humps. But men and women have brains, and they have hearts; they think and they feel,"—that will seem to it a bad joke, and an improper one into the bargain.

But to return. Here is the British public sitting by the writer's side and saying in its vast and unanimous way: "Old women have houses. They have fathers. They have incomes. They have servants. They have hot-water bottles. That is how we know that they are old women. Mr. Wells and Mr. Bennett and Mr. Galsworthy have always taught us that this is the way to recognize them. But now with your Mrs. Brown—how are we to believe in her? We do not even know whether her villa was called Albert or Balmoral; what she paid for her gloves; or whether her mother died of cancer or of consumption. How can she be alive? No; she is a mere figment of your imagination."

And old women of course ought to be made of freehold villas and copyhold estates, not of imagination.

The Georgian novelist, therefore, was in an awkward predicament. There was Mrs. Brown protesting that she was different, quite different, from what people made out, and luring the novelist to her rescue by the most fascinating if fleeting glimpse of her charms; there were the Edwardians handing out tools appropriate to house building and house breaking; and there was the British public asseverating that they must see the hot-water bottle first. Meanwhile the train was rushing to the station where we must all get out.

Such, I think, was the predicament in which the young Georgians found themselves about the year 1910. Many of them—I am thinking of Mr. Forster and Mr. Lawrence in particular—spoilt their early work because, instead of throwing away those tools, they tried to use them. They tried to compromise. They tried to combine their own direct sense of the oddity and significance of some character with Mr. Galsworthy's knowledge of the Factory Acts, and Mr. Bennett's knowledge of the Five Towns. They tried it, but they had too keen, too overpowering a sense of Mrs. Brown and her peculiarities to go on trying it much longer. Something had to be done. At whatever cost to life, limb, and damage to valuable property Mrs. Brown must be rescued, expressed, and set in her high relations to the world before the train stopped and she disappeared for ever. And so the smashing and the crashing began. Thus it is that we hear all round us, in poems and novels and biographies, even in newspaper articles and essays, the sound of breaking and falling, crashing and destruction. It is the prevailing sound of the Georgian age—rather a melancholy one if you think what melodius days there have been in the past, if you think of Shakespeare and Milton and Keats or even of Jane Austen and Thackeray and Dickens; if you think of the language, and the heights to which it can soar when free, and see the same eagle captive, bald, and croaking.

In view of these facts—with these sounds in my ears and these fancies in my brain—I am not going to deny that Mr. Bennett has some reason when he complains that our Georgian writers are unable to make us believe that our characters are real. I am forced to agree that they do not pour out three immortal masterpieces with Victorian regularity every autumn. But, instead of being gloomy, I am sanguine. For this state of things is, I think, inevitable whenever from hoar old age or callow youth the convention ceases to be a means of communication between writer and reader, and becomes instead an obstacle and an impediment. At the present moment we are suffering, not from decay, but from having no code of manners which writers and readers accept as a prelude to the more exciting intercourse of friendship. The literary convention of the time is so artificial—you have to talk about the weather and nothing but the weather throughout the entire visit—that, naturally, the feeble are tempted to outrage, and the strong are led to destroy the very foundations and rules of literary society. Signs of this are everywhere apparent. Grammar is violated; syntax disintegrated; as a boy staying with an aunt for the week-end rolls in the geranium bed out of sheer desperation as the solemnities of the sabbath wear on. The more adult writers do not, of course, indulge in such wanton exhibitions of spleen. Their sincerity is desperate, and their courage tremendous; it is only that they do not know which to use, a fork or their fingers. Thus, if you read Mr. Joyce and Mr. Eliot you will be struck by the indecency of the one, and the obscurity of the other. Mr. Joyce's indecency in *Ulysses* seems to me the conscious and calculated indecency of a desperate man who feels that in order to breathe he must break the window. At moments, when the window is broken, he is magnificent. But what a waste of energy! And, after all, how dull indecency is, when it is not the overflowing of a superabundant energy or savagery, but the determined and public-spirited act of a man who needs fresh air! Again, with the obscurity of Mr. Eliot. I think that Mr. Eliot has written some of the loveliest single lines in modern poetry. But how intolerant he is of the old usages and politenesses of society—respect for the weak, consideration for the dull! As I sun myself upon the intense and ravishing beauty of one of his lines, and reflect that I must make a dizzy and dangerous leap to the next, and so on from line to line, like an acrobat flying precariously from bar to bar, I cry out, I confess, for the old decorums, and envy the indolence of my ancestors who, instead of spinning madly through mid-air, dreamt quietly in the shade with a book. Again, in Mr. Strachey's books, *Eminent Victorians* and *Queen Victoria*, the effort and strain of writing against the grain and current of the times is visible too. It is much less visible, of course, for not only is he dealing with facts, which are stubborn things, but he has fabricated, chiefly from eighteenth-century material, a very discreet code of manners of his own, which allows him to sit at the table with the highest in the land and to say a great many things under cover of that exquisite apparel which, had they gone naked, would have been chased by the men-servants from the room. Still, if you compare *Eminent Victorians* with some of Lord Macaulay's essays, though you will feel that Lord Macaulay is always wrong, and Mr. Strachey always right, you will also feel a body, a sweep, a richness in Lord Macaulay's essays which show that his age was behind him; all his strength went straight into his work; none was used for purposes of concealment or of conversion. But Mr. Strachey has had to open our eyes before he made us see; he has had to search out and sew together a very artful manner of speech; and the effort, beautifully though it is concealed, has robbed his work of some of the force that should have gone into it, and limited his scope.

For these reasons, then, we must reconcile ourselves to a season of failures and fragments. We must reflect that where so much strength is spent on finding a way of telling the truth, the truth itself is bound to reach us in rather an exhausted and chaotic condition. Ulysses, Queen Victoria, Mr. Prufrock—to give Mrs. Brown some of the names she has made famous lately—is a little pale and dishevelled by the time her rescuers reach her. And it is the sound of their axes that we hear—a vigorous and stimulating sound in my ears—unless of course you wish to sleep, when, in the bounty of his concern, Providence has provided a host of writers anxious and able to satisfy your needs.

Thus I have tried, at tedious length, I fear, to answer some of the questions which I began by asking. I have given an account of some of the difficulties which in my view beset the Georgian writer in all his forms. I have sought to excuse him. May I end by venturing to remind you of the duties and responsibilities that are yours as partners in this business of writing books, as companions in the railway carriage, as fellow travellers with Mrs. Brown? For she is just as visible to you who remain silent as to us who tell stories about her. In the course of your daily life this past week you have had far stranger and more interesting experiences than the one I have tried to describe. You have overheard scraps of talk that filled you with amazement. You have gone to bed at night bewildered by the complexity of your feelings. In one day thousands of ideas have coursed through your brains; thousands of emotions have met, collided, and disappeared in astonishing disorder. Nevertheless, you allow the writers to palm off upon you a version of all this, an image of Mrs. Brown, which has no likeness to that surprising apparition whatsoever. In your modesty you seem to consider that writers are of different blood and bone from yourselves; that they know more of Mrs. Brown than you do. Never was there a more fatal mistake. It is this division between reader and writer, this humility on your part, these professional airs and graces on ours, that corrupt and emasculate the books which should be the healthy offspring of a close and equal alliance between us. Hence spring those sleek, smooth novels, those portentous and ridiculous biographies, that milk and watery criticism, those poems melodiously celebrating the innocence of roses and sheep which pass so plausibly for literature at the present time.

Your part is to insist that writers shall come down off their plinths and pedestals, and describe beautifully if possible, truthfully at any rate, our Mrs. Brown. You should insist that she is an old lady of unlimited capacity and infinite variety; capable of appearing in any place; wearing any dress; saying anything and doing heaven knows what. But the things she says and the things she does and her eyes and her nose and her speech and her silence have an overwhelming fascination, for she is, of course, the spirit we live by, life itself.

But do not expect just at present a complete and satisfactory presentment of her. Tolerate the spasmodic, the obscure, the fragmentary, the failure. Your help is invoked in a good cause. For I will make one final and surpassingly rash prediction—we are trembling on the verge of one of the great ages of English literature. But it can only be reached if we are determined never, never to desert Mrs. Brown.

Modern Fiction

In making any survey, even the freest and loosest, of modern fiction, it is difficult not to take it for granted that the modern practice of the art is somehow an improvement upon the old. With their simple tools and primitive materials, it might be said, Fielding did well and Jane Austen even better, but compare their opportunities with ours! Their masterpieces certainly have a strange air of simplicity. And yet the analogy between literature and the process, to choose an example, of making motor cars scarcely holds good beyond the first glance. It is doubtful whether in the course of the centuries, though we have learnt much about making machines, we have learnt anything about making literature. We do not come to write better; all that we can be said to do is to keep moving, now a little in this direction, now in that, but with a circular tendency should the whole course of the track be viewed from a sufficiently lofty pinnacle. It need scarcely be said that we make no claim to stand, even momentarily, upon that vantage-ground. On the flat, in the crowd, half blind with dust, we look back with envy to those happier warriors, whose battle is won and whose achievements wear so serene an air of accomplishment that we can scarcely refrain from whispering that the fight was not so fierce for them as for us. It is for the historian of literature to decide; for him to say if we are now beginning or ending or standing in the middle of a great period of prose fiction, for down in the plain little is visible. We only know that certain gratitudes and hostilities inspire us; that certain paths seem to lead to fertile land, others to the dust and the desert; and of this perhaps it may be worth while to attempt some account.

Our quarrel, then, is not with the classics, and if we speak of quarrelling with Mr. Wells, Mr. Bennett, and Mr. Galsworthy, it is partly that by the mere fact of their existence in the flesh their work has a living, breathing, everyday imperfection which bids us take what liberties with it we choose. But it is also true that, while we thank them for a thousand gifts, we reserve our unconditional gratitude for Mr. Hardy, for Mr. Conrad, and in much lesser degree for the Mr. Hudson of *The Purple Land, Green Mansions,* and *Far Away and Long Ago.* Mr. Wells, Mr. Bennett, and Mr. Galsworthy have excited so many hopes and disappointed them so persistently that our gratitude largely takes the form of thinking them for having shown us what they might have done but have not done; what we certainly could not do, but as certainly, perhaps, do not wish to do. No single phrase will sum up the charge or grievance which we have to bring against a mass of work so large in its volume and embodying so many qualities, both admirable and the reverse. If we tried to formulate our meaning in one word we should say that these three writers are materialists. It is because they are concerned not with the spirit but with the body that they have disappointed us, and left us with the feeling that the sooner English fiction turns its back upon them, as politely as may be, and marches, if only into the desert, the better for its soul. Naturally, no single word reaches the centre of three separate targets. In the case of Mr. Wells it falls notably wide of the mark. And yet even with him it indicates to our thinking the fatal alloy in his genius, the great clod of clay that has got itself mixed up with the purity of his inspiration. But Mr. Bennett is perhaps the worst culprit of the three, inasmuch as he is by far the best workman. He can make a book so well constructed and solid in its craftsmanship that it is difficult for the most exacting of critics to see through what chink or crevice decay can creep in. There is not so much as a draught between the frames of the windows, or a crack in the boards. And yet—if life should refuse to live there? That is a risk which the creator of *The Old Wives' Tale,* George Cannon, Edwin Clayhanger, and hosts of other figures, may well claim to have surmounted. His characters live abundantly, even unexpectedly, but it remains to ask how do they live, and what do they live for? More and more they seem to us, deserting even the well-built villa in the Five Towns, to spend their time in some softly padded first-class railway carriage, pressing bells and buttons innumerable; and the destiny to which they travel so luxuriously becomes more and more unquestionably an eternity of bliss spent in the very best hotel in Brighton. It can scarcely be said of Mr. Wells that he is a materialist in the sense that he takes too much delight in the solidity of his fabric. His mind is too generous in its sympathies to allow him to spend much time in making things ship-shape and substantial. He is a materialist from sheer goodness of heart, taking upon his shoulders the work that ought to have been discharged by Government officials, and in the plethora of his ideas and facts scarcely having leisure to realize, or forgetting to think important, the crudity and coarseness of his human beings. Yet what more damaging criticism can there be both of his earth and of his Heaven than that they are to be inhabited here and hereafter by his Joans and his Peters? Does not the inferiority of their natures tarnish whatever institutions and ideals may be provided for them by the generosity of their creator? Nor, profoundly though we respect the integrity and humanity of Mr. Galsworthy, shall we find what we seek in his pages.

If we fasten, then, one label on all these books, on which is one word, materialists, we mean by it that they write of unimportant things; they they spend immense skill and immense industry making the trivial and the transitory appear the true and the enduring.

We have to admit that we are exacting, and, further, that we find it difficult to justify our discontent by explaining what it is that we exact. We frame our question differently at different times. But it reappears most persistently as we drop the finished novel on the crest of a sigh— Is it worth while? What is the point of it all? Can it be that, owing to one of those little deviations which the human spirit seems to make from time to time, Mr. Bennett has come down with his magnificant apparatus for catching life just an inch or two on the wrong side? Life escapes; and perhaps without life nothing else is worth while. It is a confession of vagueness to have to make use of such a figure as this, but we scarcely better the matter by speaking, as critics are prone to do, of reality. Admitting the vagueness which afflicts all criticism of novels, let us hazard the opinion that for us at this moment the form of fiction most in vogue more often misses than secures the thing we seek. Whether we call it life or spirit, truth or reality, this, the essential thing, has moved off, or on, and refuses to be contained any longer in such ill-fitting vestments as we provide. Nevertheless, we go on perseveringly, conscientiously, constructing our two and thirty chapters after a design which more and more ceases to resemble the vision in our minds. So much of the enormous labour of proving the solidity, the likeness to life, of the story is not merely labour thrown away but labour misplaced to the extent of obscuring and blotting out the light of the conception. The writer seems constrained, not by his own free will but by some powerful and unscrupulous tyrant who has him in thrall, to provide a plot, to provide comedy, tragedy, love interest, and an air

98

of probability embalming the whole so impeccable that if all his figures were to come to life they would find themselves dressed down to the last button of their coats in the fashion of the hour. The tyrant is obeyed; the novel is done to a turn. But sometimes, more and more often as time goes by, we suspect a momentary doubt, a spasm of rebellion, as the pages fill themselves in the customary way. Is life like this? Must novels be like this?

Look within and life, it seems, is very far from being "like this." Examine for a moment an ordinary mind on an ordinary day. The mind receives a myriad impressions—trivial, fantastic, evanescent, or engraved with the sharpness of steel. From all sides they come, an incessant shower of innumerable atoms; and as they fall, as they shape themselves into the life of Monday or Tuesday, the accent falls differently from of old; the moment of importance came not here but there; so that, if a writer were a free man and not a slave, if he could write what he chose, not what he must, if he could base his work upon his own feeling and not upon convention, there would be no plot, no comedy, no tragedy, no love interest or catastrophe in the accepted style, and perhaps not a single button sewn on as the Bond Street tailors would have it. Life is not a series of gig-lamps symmetrically arranged; life is a luminous halo, a semi-transparent envelope surrounding us from the beginning of consciousness to the end. Is it not the task of the novelist to convey this varying, this unknown and uncircumscribed spirit, whatever aberration or complexity it may display, with as little mixture of the alien and external as possible? We are not pleading merely for courage and sincerity; we are suggesting that the proper stuff of fiction is a little other than custom would have us believe it.

It is, at any rate, in some such fashion as this that we seek to define the quality which distinguishes the work of several young writers, among whom Mr. James Joyce is the most notable, from that of their predecessors. They attempt to come closer to life, and to preserve more sincerely and exactly what interests and moves them, even if to do so they must discard most of the conventions which are commonly observed by the novelist. Let us record the atoms as they fall upon the mind in the order in which they fall, let us trace the pattern, however disconnected and incoherent in appearance, which each sight or incident scores upon the consciousness. Let us not take it for granted that life exists more fully in what is commonly thought big than in what is commonly thought small. Anyone who has read *A Portrait of the Artist as a Young Man* or, what promises to be a far more interesting work,

The Writer

Ulysses, now appearing in the [April 1919] *Little Review*, will have hazarded some theory of this nature as to Mr. Joyce's intention. On our part, with such a fragment before us, it is hazarded rather than affirmed; but whatever the intention of the whole, there can be no question but that it is of the utmost sincerity and that the result, difficult or unpleasant as we may judge it, is undeniably important. In contrast with those whom we have called materialists, Mr. Joyce is spiritual; he is concerned at all costs to reveal the flickerings of that innermost flame which flashes its messages through the brain, and in order to preserve it he disregards with complete courage whatever seems to him adventitious, whether it be probability, or coherence, or any other of these signposts which for generations have served to support the imagination of a reader when called upon to imagine what he can neither touch nor see. The scene in the cemetery, for instance, with its brilliancy, its sordidity, its incoherence, its sudden lightning flashes of significance, does undoubtedly come so close to the quick of the mind that, on a first reading at any rate, it is difficult not to acclaim a masterpiece. If we want life itself, here surely we have it. Indeed, we find ourselves fumbling rather awkwardly if we try to say what else we wish, and for what reason a work of such originality yet fails to compare, for we must take high examples, with *Youth* or *The Mayor of Casterbridge*. It fails because of the comparative poverty of the writer's mind, we might say simply and have done with it. But it is possible to press a little further and wonder whether we may not refer our sense of being in a bright yet narrow room, confined and shut in, rather than enlarged and set free, to some limitation imposed by the method as well as by the mind. Is it the method that inhibits the creative power? Is it due to the method that we feel neither jovial nor magnanimous, but centred in a self which, in spite of its tremor of susceptibility, never embraces or creates what is outside itself and beyond? Does the emphasis laid, perhaps didactically, upon indecency contribute to the effect of something angular and isolated? Or is it merely that in any effort of such originality it is much easier, for contemporaries especially, to feel what it lacks than to name what it gives? In any case it is a mistake to stand outside examining "methods." Any method is right, every method is right, that expresses what we wish to express, if we are writers; that brings us closer to the novelist's intention if we are readers. This method has the merit of bringing us closer to what we were prepared to call life itself; did not the reading of *Ulysses* suggest how much of life is excluded or ignored, and did it not come with a shock to open *Tristram*

Shandy or even *Pendennis* and be by them convinced that there are not only other aspects of life, but more important ones into the bargain.

However this may be, the problem before the novelist at present, as we supose it to have been in the past, is to contrive means of being free to set down what he chooses. He has to have the courage to say that what interests him is no longer "this" but "that": out of "that" alone must he construct his work. For the moderns "that," the point of interest, lies very likely in the dark places of psychology. At once, therefore, the accent falls a little differently; the emphasis is upon something hitherto ignored; at once a different outline of form becomes necessary, difficult for us to grasp, incomprehensible to our predecessors. No one but a modern, no one perhaps but a Russian, would have felt the interest of the situation which Tchekov has made into the short story which he calls "Gusev." Some Russian soldiers lie ill on board a ship which is taking them back to Russia. We are given a few scraps of their talk and some of their thoughts; then one of them dies and is carried away; the talk goes on among the others for a time, until Gusev himself dies, and looking "like a carrot or a radish" is thrown overboard. The emphasis is laid upon such unexpected places that at first it seems as if there were no emphasis at all; and then, as the eyes accustom themselves to twilight and discern the shapes of things in a room we see how complete the story is, how profound, and how truly in obedience to his vision Tchekov has chosen this, that, and the other, and placed them together to compose something new. But it is impossible to say "this is comic," or "that is tragic," nor are we certain, since short stories, we have been taught, should be brief and conclusive, whether this, which is vague and inconclusive, should be called a short story at all.

The most elementary remarks upon modern English fiction can hardly avoid some mention of the Russian influence, and if the Russians are mentioned one runs the risk of feeling that to write of any fiction save theirs is waste of time. If we want understanding of the soul and heart where else shall we find it of comparable profundity? If we are sick of our own materialism the least considerable of their novelists has by right of birth a natural reverence for the human spirit. "Learn to make yourself akin to people. . . . But let this sympathy be not with the mind—for it is easy with the mind—but with the heart, with love towards them." In every great Russian writer we seem to discern the features of a saint, if sympathy for the sufferings of others, love towards them, endeavour to reach some goal worthy of the most exacting demands of the spirit constitute saintliness. It is the saint in them which confounds us with a feeling of our own irreligious triviality, and turns so many of our famous novels to tinsel and trickery. The conclusions of the Russian mind, thus comprehensive and compassionate, are inevitably, perhaps, of the utmost sadness. More accurately indeed we might speak of the inconclusiveness of the Russian mind. It is the sense that there is no answer. that if honestly examined life presents question after question which must be left to sound on and on after the story is over in hopeless interrogation that fills us with a deep, and finally it may be with a resentful, despair. They are right perhaps; unquestionably they see further than we do and without our gross imediments of vision. But perhaps we see something that escapes them, or why should this voice of protest mix itself with our gloom? The voice of protest is the voice of another and an ancient civilization which seems to have bred in us the instinct to enjoy and fight rather than to suffer and understand. English fiction from Sterne to Meredith bears witness to our natural delight in humour and comedy, in the beauty of earth, in the activities of the intellect, and in the splendour of the body. But any deductions that we may draw from the comparison of two fictions so immeasurably far apart are futile save indeed as they flood us with a view of the infinite possibilities of the art and remind us that there is no limit to the horizon, and that nothing—no "method," no experiment, even of the wildest—is forbidden, but only falsity and pretence. "The proper stuff of fiction" does not exist; everything is the proper stuff of fiction, every feeling, every thought; every quality of brain and spirit is drawn upon; no perception comes amiss. And if we can imagine the art of fiction come alive and standing in our midst, she would undoubtedly bid us break her and bully her, as well as honour and love her, for so her youth is renewed and her sovereignty assured.

Part 3

THE CRITICS

Introduction

The essays collected here were chosen for their intrinsic merit and also because they are relatively brief but complete studies not available elsewhere in book form. They range widely in approach and method, sometimes taking positions quite different from those of this writer. That is as it should be: criticism flourishes on controversy, and more is learned from disagreement than from agreement.

Katherine Mansfield's essay (1919) was among the many favorable reviews to greet the appearance of "Kew Gardens." Edward L. Bishop quotes from other contemporary reviews, but Mansfield's is particularly interesting because it offers the insights of a practicing writer. It is more an appreciation than an analysis, contrasting Virginia Woolf's craft with the then-current fashion (as Mansfield saw it) for subjective formlessness. Mansfield then goes on to describe Woolf's apparent indifference in the story to human beings, until the triumphant finale directs our attention to the whole pattern, human and nonhuman, created by the story. Edward L. Bishop's study of the same story sees it as an application of the theory propounded in "Modern Fiction." He emphasizes the story's atmosphere and its attempt to fix momentarily in words the shifting, shimmering reality of the external world. The "it" being pursued is "the essence of the natural and the human world of the garden."

In sharp contrast to the painterly effects of "Kew Gardens" is the "allegory," as Robert Watson calls it, of "Solid Objects." In Watson's suggestive analysis, John represents the contemplative life, his friend Charles the active life. In turn, John's obsessive collecting of bits of glass, pottery, and iron becomes an allegory of Woolf's own creative processes and of her chilly relations to the things of this world.

A very different critical approach to a very different kind of story is found in Victor de Araujo's close, New Critical reading of "A Haunted House." De Araujo interprets this tender, wistful story as depicting communication between the living and the dead, the past and the present, which leads to the insight by the living couple in the story that true buried treasure is not material but "the light in the heart."

In contrast to this very private and inward story is the group known as the "party" stories. Frank Baldanza traces what Woolf herself called the "party consciousness" through these connected stories and several of the novels. "Party consciousness" is one of the many states of heightened awareness that lead to moments of insight and revelation. Baldanza identifies this trait in Clarissa Dalloway and in other of Woolf's characters and relates it to the philosophy of G. E. Moore, which influenced many members of the Bloomsbury set to which Virginia Woolf belonged.

Finally, analyzing one of several of Woolf's stories in which one character imaginatively re-creates the life of another, James Hafley examines "Moments of Being: 'Slater's Pins Have No Points.'" Hafley emphasizes that Fanny Wilmot's "insight" into the life of her teacher, Julia Craye, resembles in method the story we are reading. That is, what Fanny creates is not "the truth" but a work of art, an imaginative creation—ambiguous and in many ways false, whatever its intensity.

These essays require no further introduction, save for one technical point. Since Susan Dick's edition of *The Complete Shorter Fiction of Virginia Woolf* is the source for all quotations from the stories in the first part of this book, the same text has been used for these essays. Thus, page numbers of citations in these essays appear in square brackets to indicate the editorial change. This should make references to the stories easy to locate in a single source.

A Short Story:
"Kew Gardens" by Virginia Woolf
Katherine Mansfield*

If it were not a matter to sigh over, it would be almost amusing to remember how short a time has passed since Samuel Butler advised the budding author to keep a notebook. What would be the author's reply to such a counsel nowadays but an amused smile: "I keep nothing else!" True; but if we remember rightly, Samuel Butler goes a little further; he suggests that the notebook should be kept in the pocket, and that is what the budding author finds intolerably hard. Up till now he has been so busy growing and blowing that his masterpieces still are unwritten, but there are the public waiting, gaping. Hasn't he anything to offer before they wander elsewhere? Can't he startle their attention by sheer roughness and crudeness and general slapdashery? Out comes the note-book, and the deed is done. And since they find its contents absolutely thrilling and satisfying, is it to be wondered at that the risk of producing anything bigger, more solid, and more positive—is not taken? The note-books of young writers are their laurels; they prefer to rest on them. It is here that one begins to sigh, for it is here that the young author begins to swell and to demand that, since he has chosen to make his note-books his All, they shall be regarded as of the first importance, read with a deadly seriousness and acclaimed as a kind of new Art—the art of not taking pains, of never wondering why it was one fell in love with this or that, but contenting oneself with the public's dreary interest in promiscuity.

Perhaps that is why one feels that Mrs. Virginia Woolf's story belongs to another age. It is so far removed from the note-book literature of our day, so exquisite an example of love at second sight. She begins where the others leave off, entering Kew Gardens, as it were, alone and at her leisure when their little first screams of excitement have died away and they have rushed afield to some new brilliant joy. It is strange how conscious one is, from the first paragraph, of this sense of leisure; her

*Reprinted from *Novels & Novelists*, ed. J. Middleton Murry (Boston: Beacon Hill, 1930), 36–38.

story is bathed in it as if it were a light, still and lovely, heightening the importance of everything, and filling all that is within her vision with that vivid, disturbing beauty that haunts the air the last moment before sunset or the first moment after dawn. Poise—yes, poise. Anything may happen; her world is on tiptoe.

This is her theme. In Kew Gardens there was a flowerbed full of red and blue and yellow flowers. Through the hot July afternoon men and women "straggled past the flower-bed with a curiously irregular movement not unlike that of the white and blue butterflies who crossed the turf in zig-zag flights from bed to bed," paused for a moment, were "caught" in its dazzling net, and then moved on again and were lost. The mysterious intricate life of the flower-bed goes on untouched by these odd creatures. A little wind moves, stirring the petals so that their colours shake on to the brown earth, grey of a pebble, shell of a snail, a raindrop, a leaf, and for a moment the secret life is half-revealed; then a wind blows again, and the colours flash in the air and there are only leaves and flowers. . . .

It happens so often—or so seldom—in life, as we move among the trees, up and down the known and unknown paths, across the lawns and into the shade and out again, that something—for no reason that we can discover—gives us pause. Why is it that, thinking back upon that July afternoon, we see so distinctly that flower-bed? We must have passed myriads of flowers that day; why do these particular ones return? It is true, we stopped in front of them, and talked a little and then moved on. But, though we weren't conscious of it at the time, something was happening—something. . . .

But it would seem that the author, with her wise smile, is as indifferent as the flowers to these odd creatures and their ways. The tiny rich minute life of a snail—how she describes it! the angular high-stepping green insect—how passionate is her concern for him! Fascinated and credulous, we believe these things are all her concern until suddenly with a gesture she shows us the flower-bed, growing, expanding in the heat and light, filling a whole world.

(June 13, 1919)

Pursuing "It" through "Kew Gardens"

*Edward L. Bishop**

> "Lucky it isn't Friday," he observed.
> "Why? D'you believe in luck?"
> "They make you pay sixpence on Friday."
> "What's sixpence anyway? Isn't it worth sixpence?"
> "What's 'it'—what do you mean by 'it'?"
> "O, anything—I mean—you know what I mean."

The reader knows what the young woman means because the conversation occurs near the close of "Kew Gardens" and Virginia Woolf has already captured "it": the essence of the natural and the human world of the garden. From the beginning of her career Woolf had been pursuing the "uncircumscribed spirit" of life, but she had been frustrated by the methods of conventional fiction. Now, she makes no attempt to deal with "it" discursively—she does not, as she might have done in *The Voyage Out,* have a pair of sensitive individuals discuss the "whatness" of Kew.[1] Neither does she offer straightforward description. The sketch represents the artistic application of Woolf's famous manifesto published only the month before in her essay "Modern Fiction": "Life is not a series of gig-lamps symmetrically arranged: life is a luminous halo, a semi-transparent envelope surrounding us from the beginning of consciousness to the end."[2] In "Kew Gardens" Woolf does not document the physical scene, she immerses the reader in the atmosphere of the garden.

Her success in the piece was immediately recognized. Harold Child, writing in [the *Times Literary Supplement*] on the first appearance of "Kew Gardens" (1919) lauded this "new proof of the complete unimportance in art of the *hyle,* the subject matter":

> Titian paints Bacchus and Ariadne; and Rembrandt paints a hideous old woman. . . . And Mrs. Woolf writes about Kew Gardens and a snail and some stupid people. But here is "Kew Gardens"—a work of art, made, "created," as we say, finished, four-square; a thing of original and therefore strange beauty, with its own "atmosphere," its own vital force.[3]

*Reprinted by permission from *Studies in Short Fiction* 19 (1982):269–75.

Subsequent writers have agreed with Child, notice that the source of the sketch's vitality lies in the linguistic strategies of the narrating consciousness. In an early study (1942), David Daiches writes, "The author's reverie is what organizes the images and the characters; and an intellectual play uses the images as starting points for meditation."[4] James Hafley, in his exploration of the Bergsonian concepts in Woolf's fiction (1954), argues that the sketch is about "life" in the Bergsonian sense, a "vital impetus" that is not logically explicable, and which must be "first directly apprehended and then crippled into words." But what is contradictory in Bergson is, Hafley claims, "supremely consistent and translucent" in Woolf.[5] In the next decade (1965) Guiget focussed on the method of the piece, observing that "as the eye traces an imagined arabesque through this mosaic, the mind regroups fresh wholes in this atomized universe, breaks habitual links and associations to form others, hitherto unnoticed or neglected."[6] In a recent consideration of Woolf's narrators (1980) Hafley returns to "Kew Gardens," locating the "vital force" in the language itself, not in any specific quality of imagery but in the action of the voice. In the sketch narration becomes "creation rather than transmission."[7] Yet precisely *how* this is achieved, how the mind is led to "regroup fresh wholes," how the "luminous halo" is generated, has never been adequately demonstrated. And it is only by looking very closely at the way the language operates that we can see how Woolf simultaneously creates and engages the reader with something as nebulous as an "atmosphere."

To glance first at the most obvious strategies of narration, in "Kew Gardens" Woolf dispenses with the carefully articulated structures of *Night and Day,* the "scaffolding" as she calls it.[8] There is very little external action here—a series of couples strolls past a flower bed in which a snail is struggling to get past a leaf—and the development seems as "aimless and irregular" as the movements of the people in the gardens. On closer examination it becomes obvious that the sketch is carefully constructed: there are four couples and among them they constitute a cross-section of social class (middle, upper, and lower), age (maturity, old age, and youth) and relation (husband and wife, male companions, female friends, lovers); and their appearances are neatly interspersed among four passages which describe the action in the flower bed. Yet this pattern is not insisted upon; the juxtapositions are not abrupt or pointed. As in her later works, the progression of events (the "series of gig-lamps") has been subordinated to the modulation of emotion, and the ending conveys a sense of resolution more than of narrative conclusion. In the human encounters too a similarly under-stated order obtains. The pleasantly elegiac mood created by the mar-ried couple, Eleanor and Simon, gives way to uneasy tension as the old man exhibits a senility that borders on madness. The glimpse of something darker merely hints at the turmoil underlying the tranquil scene (a conjunction of beauty and terror that remains constant in Woolf's writings) before the coarse curiosity of the two women restores the lighter tone. Finally the emotions that the lovers now feel echo those evoked in Eleanor and Simon only by their memories. Thus Woolf quietly comes full circle to end with love, before shifting to a more encompassing vision of unity—the entelechy of all her works—of human beings integrated not just with each other but with the phe-nomenal world: "they wavered and sought shade beneath the trees, dissolving like drops of water in the yellow and green atmosphere, staining it faintly with red and blue" [*CS*, 89].[9]

The achieved effect of the sketch, the sense that it is an atmosphere into which one moves, follows in part from the fluid overall structure, but the reader's immersion begins at the outset with the smoothly shifting point of view. Woolf does more than set the scene in the open-ing paragraph, she smoothly dislocates the reader's accustomed per-spective of a landscape. The first sentence, "From the oval-shaped flower-bed there rose perhaps a hundred stalks . . . "[*CS*, 84], begins with a description from a middle distance; the narrator sees the shape of the bed as a whole, but also sees the flowers as individual entities, not as a solid mass. Yet by the end of the sentence the narrator has moved much closer, to the "yellow gloom of the throat," from which emerges "a straight bar, rough with gold dust and slightly clubbed at the end." And, as the light "move[s] on and spread[s] its illumination in the *vast* green spaces" (my italics) beneath the dome of leaves, the reader has been placed among the flowers and given a correspondingly different sense of scale. As the paragraph closes, the breeze "over-head" is above him in the petals, not in the trees: "Then the breeze stirred rather more briskly overhead and the colour was flashed into the air above, into the eyes of the men and women. . . . " The reader now finds himself viewing the bed from within—his angle of vision is in fact that of the snail—rather than admiring the floral designs as a more distant observer.

Just as the initial description begins with and then moves beyond a conventional perspective on the scene, so the first exchange between Eleanor and Simon ("'Fifteen years ago I came here with Lily,' he thought. . . . 'Tell me, Eleanor. D'you ever think of the past?'") moves out of interior monologue and then, with "'For me, a square silver shoe buckle and a dragon fly—' 'For me, a kiss . . .'" [*CS*, 84–85] into a new mode, one that seems to combine qualities of both thought and speech. Again, Woolf is gently forcing the reader out of his established perceptual habits, raising questions about the nature of discourse and the conventions used to render it. And, just as she has placed the reader within the garden, so with each successive dialogue she moves deeper, below the flat surface of words, to reveal that, like the apparently flat flower-bed, language too has cliffs and hollows. In doing so she dramatizes the way in which one often perceives words less as units of information than as physical sensation. Indeed, as the two women talk, their words finally cease to have more than vestigial denotative meaning for the "stout" member of the pair; they become as palpable, and as non-cognitive, as a rain shower: "The ponderous woman looked through the pattern of falling words at the flowers. . . . She stood there letting the words fall over her, swaying the top part of her body slowly backwards and forwards, looking at the flowers" [*CS*, 87]. The image prepares the reader for the final encounter, that between Trissie and her young man. For after the brief discussion on the cost of admission (quoted at the beginning of this essay) Woolf moves into their minds, exploring the unvoiced reactions to their colloquy. It is here that the alternation between description and dialogue becomes a fusion, as the words become not merely a "pattern" but a contoured landscape, and one whose features echo those of the terrain through which the snail has been moving.

In this episode Woolf displays what will become the defining characteristic of her later prose: a flexible narrative style which allows her to move without obvious transition from an external point of view to one within the mind of a character, and back again, thus fusing the physical setting with the perceiving consciousness.[10] Further, it is a mode which invites the reader's participation in the process, so that the reality Woolf conveys is apprehended through the experience of reading. In the passage quoted below, the reader becomes conscious of moving *among* words, just as the characters do.

> Long pauses came between each of these remarks; they were uttered in toneless and monotonous voices. The couple stood still on the edge of the flower bed, and together pressed the end of her

parasol deep down into the soft earth. The action and the fact that his hand rested on the top of hers expressed their feelings in a strange way, as these short insignificant words also expressed something, words with short wings for their heavy body of meaning, inadequate to carry *them* far and thus alighting awkwardly upon the very common objects that surrounded *them*, and were to *their* inexperienced touch so massive; but who knows (so they thought as they pressed the parasol into the earth) what precipices aren't concealed in *them*, or what slopes of ice don't shine in the sun on the other side? Who knows? Who has ever seen this before? Even when she wondered what sort of tea they gave you at Kew, he felt that something loomed up behind her words, and stood vast and solid behind them; and the mist very slowly rose and uncovered—O, Heavens, what were those shapes?—little white tables, and waitresses. . . .
[*CS*, 88; Bishop's italics]

The passage begins straightforwardly enough: the narrator notes the pauses, the tone of the remarks, the posture of the couple. But in the third sentence, as she explores the relation of the words to the feelings they are meant to convey, the narrator draws the reader into the emotions of the couple. The initial image describing the words evolves into an extended metaphor that communicates more exactly the "something" the young couple feels, and the metaphor works in part through deliberately ambiguous pronouns which both enforce the reader's engagement and unite the disparate elements of the scene.

The words "with short wings for their heavy body . . . " suggest bees—appropriate both to the garden and to the drone of the "toneless and monotonous voices" of the speakers. As the passage develops, it sustains this dual reference: "inadequate to carry them far" seems to refer as easily to the words being inadequate to carry the couple far as it does to the wings being inadequate to carry the words far. The latter proves to be the primary meaning, for the words alight on the "common objects." But with "common objects that surrounded *them*" the pronoun can refer to either the couple or the words. The latter would appear to be the logical choice, yet in the next clause, "and were to *their* inexperienced touch so massive," the pronoun obviously refers to the couple.

"Massive," however, seems to modify the "common objects"—in which case "their" should refer to the words-as-bees—unless the words from the couple's point of view are massive. This seems unlikely (they have been described as "short, insignificant"), and the following clause "but who knows . . . what precipices aren't concealed in them" perpetuates the confusion over the pronoun referent, for the reader knows that there are precipices in these common objects; he has already encountered the "brown cliffs and deep green lakes" [*CS*, 85–86] that block the snail's path. Nevertheless, the precipices do reside in the words. The image of the bee has somehow fallen by the way, and the young man and woman now look through the words, as the older woman earlier "looked through the pattern of falling words at the flowers," to the something "vast and solid" behind the words.

I spoke of confusion, and the passage is confusing if one insists on pinning down all the referents. But through an alert and unprejudiced attention to the syntax, one can more firmly apprehend the action of the figures: what is being fostered is identification, not confusion. The reader does not find the passage muddled; rather he experiences the sense of one thing merging with another—the couple with the words, the words with the surrounding objects. And he easily makes the transition from bees to precipices, for the one expresses the activity of the conversation, while the other conveys the young man's perception of the meaning behind the words; the massiveness and solidity express the intensity of their emotions. Indeed, the image of the bee, from "words with short wings . . . " to " . . . that surrounded them," can be regarded as a parenthetical aside by the narrator, after which she returns to the consciousness of the young couple. In any case, Woolf's supple prose ensures that while the reader is invited to attend closely he is not forced to pause. The impression of a cloudiness or "mist" that she creates derives from extreme precision, not vagueness, and it conveys exactly that sense lovers have of the world dissolving into soft focus as they become for a moment oblivious of all except each other. Further, the reader experiences the wonder at ordinary objects which follows such intense moments: "O, Heavens, what were those shapes—little white tables. . . ." Yet by using the most bathetic object available to satisfy that portentous anticipation, Woolf gently puts the event in perspective; the reader feels a sympathetic amusement toward the infatuated couple. He continues to identify with them, however, for the shock of wonder is not described, rather it is conveyed through the prose as the reader emerges from the mist of the passage.

In fact the reader is not yet fully out of the mist, for the tables and waitresses, he gradually discerns, have not been observed—they are just now taking shape in the young man's mind:

> O, Heavens, what were those shapes?—little white tables, and wait-resses who looked first at her and then at him; and there was a bill that he would pay with a real two shilling piece, and it was real, all real, he assured himself, fingering the coin in his pocket, real to everyone except to him and to her; even to him it began to seem real; and then—but it was too exciting to stand and think any longer, and he pulled the parasol out of the earth with a jerk and was im-patient to find the place where one had tea with other people, like other people. [*CS*, 88]

The touch of the coin brings him back by degrees to the external world—"even to him it began to seem real"—and the reader too must struggle to regain the conventional sense of the reality of the park. For Woolf has convinced him of what she had so firmly stated in "Modern Fiction," that life "is a little other than custom would have us believe it."[11] In any case, Woolf does not follow them to tea; the sketch closes with a vision of the human bodies, the flowers, the voices and the traffic noises all dissolving in the heat of the afternoon. The tables, the shilling, the parasol, elements she called "the alien and external," fi-nally have far less immediacy than what Trissie could only describe as "it": the "yellow and green atmosphere" that is both ethos and ambi-ence of the garden.[12]

In her fiction Woolf continued to explore the relation between language and reality—both dramatically, through the experience and conscious probing of her characters, and formally, through the ex-perimental techniques of her works. But with "Kew Gardens" she had discovered her voice, one that would remain more or less constant through the varied narrative structures she employed from *Jacob's Room* to *Between the Acts*. The quality she called "life" or the "essential thing" refused to be fixed by a phrase, but it could be arrested, briefly, by a net of words: words that evoke as well as indicate, that conspire to produce their own luminous halo, rendering (by inducing) a process of consciousness rather than a concrete picture. Thus it is that the value of her fiction derives less from the specific insights it imparts (one finds it difficult to remember the particulars of her works) than from the fact that the experience of reading initiates, in the sensitive reader, a growth of perception. We too come closer to apprehending "it" through our sojourn in "Kew Gardens."

Notes

1. Nevertheless, even in her first novel there are strong indications of the direction her writing was to take. See my discussion in "Towards the Far Side of Language: Virginia Woolf's *The Voyage Out*," *Twentieth Century Literature*, 27 (Winter 1981), 343–363.

2. *Collected Essays*, ed. Leonard Woolf (London: The Hogarth Press, 1972), II, 106.

3. "Kew Gardens," unsigned review, *Times Literary Supplement*, 29 May 1919, p. 293; rpt. *Virginia Woolf: The Critical Heritage*, ed. Robin Majumdar and Allen McLaurin (London: Routledge and Kegan Paul, 1975), p. 67.

4. David Daiches, *Virginia Woolf* (Norfolk: New Directions, 1942), pp. 50–51.

5. James Hafley, *The Glass Roof* (Berkeley: University of California Press, 1954), pp. 42–43.

6. Jean Guiget, *Virginia Woolf and Her Works*, trans. Jean Stewart (New York: Harcourt, Brace and World, 1965), p. 216.

7. James Hafley, "Virginia Woolf's Narrators and the Art of 'Life Itself'" in *Virginia Woolf: Revaluation and Continuity*, ed. Ralph Freedman (Berkeley: University of California Press, 1980), p. 42.

8. Woolf herself was quite conscious that the sketches were prototypes of her later narratives. Writing in her diary seven months after "Kew Gardens" (26 January 1920), as *Jacob's Room* was beginning to take shape, she says, "I figure that the approach will be entirely different this time: no scaffolding; scarcely a brick to be seen; . . . " and she recalls the image of the halo when she states that her goal shall be to include "the heart, the passion, humour, everything as bright as fire in the mist . . . conceive mark on the wall, K[ew]. G[ardens]. & Unwritten novel taking hands & dancing in unity." See *The Diary of Virginia Woolf, Volume II: 1920–1924*, ed. Anne Olivier Bell (London: The Hogarth Press, 1978), pp. 13–14.

9. All subsequent references are noted in the text. In his analysis of the structures of Woolf's stories, Avrom Fleishman also observes how the seeming randomness of "Kew Gardens" yields at last a satisfying unity. Citing the "closure value" of repetition, he argues that "repetition may be a means of discovery . . . the story may find at last the 'right' word . . . establish[ing] it as the articulation of the entire tale." In this case "'voices' emerges as the final and triumphant term." See "Forms of the Woolfian Short Story" in *Revaluation and Continuity*, pp. 51, 56–57. Thus even though the work is open-ended in

terms of action, there is a formal closure which gives it that "finished, four-square" look Child had remarked.

10. Also, as Hafley notes, "it is a voice famous for disappearing into the other voices it creates, especially in interior monologue." *Revaluation and Continuity*, p. 42. For a detailed discussion of the technique see Dorrit Cohn, "Narrated Monologue: Definition of a Fictional Style," *Comparative Literature*, 18 (Spring 1966), 97–112.

11. CE, II, 106. As Child attests, "We are firmly convinced of the truth of 'Kew Gardens,' and as firmly convinced that it does not matter a tram-fare whether there are any Kew Gardens, or, if so, whether they are in the least like 'Kew Gardens.'" *Critical Heritage*, pp. 66–67. See also Hafley, *Revaluation and Continuity*, p. 35.

12. For a discussion of further permutations of "it" see Fleishman, *Revaluation and Continuity*, pp. 54–55, on "Solid Objects" and "The New Dress."

"Solid Objects" as Allegory
*Robert A. Watson**

If allegory, as Angus Fletcher has suggested, depicts reality not directly but in diagrammatic form, then "Solid Objects" diagrams both technical and personal aspects of Woolf's own fiction-making, its orders and disturbances. Fletcher, whose study stresses the macrocosmic-microcosmic character of the allegorical diagram, quotes a psychoanalyst's remarks to explain its function:

> The creation of this replica of the real world makes it possible to calculate and act out in advance in this "model world" before real action is taken. . . . Words and worded concepts are shadows of things, constructed for the purpose of bringing order through trial action into the chaos of real things. The macrocosm of real things outside is reflected in the microcosm of things-representatives inside. (*Allegory, the Theory of a Symbolic Mode*, Ithaca, 1964, p. 295.)

The first few paragraphs of "Solid Objects," in which an authorial agent, a kind of disembodied perceiver, carries the action, set up the

*Reprinted by permission from "'Solid Objects' as Allegory," *Virginia Woolf Miscellany*, no. 16 (1981):3–4. © 1981 Robert A. Watson.

macrocosmic model which the remaining action, the short story's microcosm, imitates.

In the opening scene the perceiver—we might call her Woolf's "demiurge"—establishes a narrative frame, a "vast semicircle of beach" on which she observes a single object, "one small black spot." She then proceeds to anatomize the spot, finding in it first "four legs," then "two young men." The process of articulation unfolds gradually as the perceiver draws closer, observing animated gestures and details of dress, and finally brings us close enough to overhear the two men arguing about politics, a subject which fails to hold the attention of the story's protagonist John. We follow the perceiver's descent from a vague general vision to a specific one. And yet, apart from their apparent disparity of interests, the two young men remain indistinguishable from one another: both are composed of "mouths, noses, chins, little moustaches, tweed caps, rough boots, shooting coats, and check stockings."

The first few paragraphs of the story, then, pose and answer a question of poetics, namely, how does one transform opaque appearances, the solid objects of the world, into a story? The answer: Beginning with a blank ground and a single generalized object, divide, articulate, and specify in a graded succession. Yet, at this stage the two men must remain generically comparable, so that their thematic differences will show more clearly. Their behaviors will serve, in lieu of distinct physical traits, to convey these differences: Charles' stick has been "slashing the beach for a mile or so;" when his companion expresses a complete lack of interest in their talk—"politics be damned,"—Charles begins "skimming flat pieces of stone over the water," throwing away the sort of thing John will soon collect; and he is obviously still engaged by the topic which has rendered John listless and "ready to take up something new." The story has set up an antithesis between "politics" and some other theme, as yet unnamed; and it has done so in true allegorical fashion with characters who virtually personify ideas.

The first portion of the story offers three personae, the authorial perceiver, whose story consists in the discovery and articulation of the two others, John, and Charles, at this stage the nearly blank materials of a narrative. By the end of paragraph these two, active in their own right, stand ready to take up the story as the authorial perceiver retires from the scene. This transfer of powers, and the beginning of the microcosmic parallelism, occurs as John, disengaged from the conversation, starts "burrowing down, down, into the sand." There, like the authorial perceiver discovering the "small black spot," he finds "a lump of glass, so thick as to be almost opaque."

Henceforth, the collection of discarded objects comes gradually to absorb all his attention. The collection parallels the perceiver's collection of John and Charles into her narrative frame, for it provokes John to fantasize, to create his own fictive cosmos. The lump of glass, for example, inspires John to speculate on its origins and nature, and to imagine that "it was almost a precious stone. You had only to enclose it in a rim of gold, or pierce it with a wire, and it became a jewel; part of a necklace, or a dull, green light upon a finger." This lapidary speculation also speaks the language of fiction-making, which sets characters in a frame, or pierces its solid materials with a thematic thread. In effect the glass like the spot, stirs the poetic impulse; and John's imaginings, like the perceiver's, expand and grow more specific: "Perhaps after all it was really a gem; something worn by a dark Princess trailing her finger in the water as she sat in the stern of the boat and listened to the slaves singing as they rowed across the Bay. Or the oak sides of a sunk Elizabethan treasure-chest had split apart, and, rolled over and over, over and over, its emeralds had come at last to shore."

Later discoveries breed similar narratives, and as John's narration increases the parallel between the outer and inner stories grows more precise. Thus we find a "Charles" and a "John" within the collection, in the antithesis of "the china so vivid and alert, and the glass so mute and contemplative"—and in this detail we also see the key to the thematic opposition of characters: Charles personifies the active life, the public reality of the politician; John the contemplative life, the private reality of the esthete, the saint, or the writer. When John ponders the two objects, wondering how they "came to exist in the same world, let alone to stand on the same narrow strip of marble in the same room," we recognize the parallel working not only between antithetical objects and characters, but also between the "narrow strip of marble," the setting of Johns' collection, and the "vast semicircle of beach," the original setting of the macrocosmic story. Moreover, like the author's fiction which lays out its creative instruments to view, John's study displays his collecting tools, a "long stick fitted with an adaptable hook" and an "old carpet bag"—items suggesting the author's probing imagination and consolidating memory.

But despite all the parallels which seem to affirm the value of creative imagination, John's story disturbs us. He becomes strange and obsessive, gradually isolating himself: "People gave up visiting him.

He never talked to anyone about his serious ambitions; their lack of understanding was apparent in their behavior." If John's story involves an allegorical debate won by the contemplative over the active principle, by the esthetic over the political vision, it also hints at the disturbing consequence of such creative eccentricity. The sense of disharmony John's privacy entails surfaces through another item of the collection, namely:

> . . . a very remarkable piece of iron. It was almost identical with the glass in shape, massy and globular, but so cold and heavy, so black and metallic, that it was evidently alien to earth and had its origin in one of the dead stars or was itself a cinder of the moon. It weighed the pocket down; it weighed the mantelpiece down; it radiated cold. And yet the meteorite stood upon the same ledge with the lump of glass and the star-shaped china.

His microcosmic collection and the author's macrocosmic narrative acquire their "anti-cosmos" in this too-solid object, the coldness of which, when we consider the end of Woolf's personal dialogue with the world, radiates the more ominously.

"Solid Objects," in short, diagrams not only a fictional technique, but also the author's odd relations with the things of the world, the interpretive relations that produce stories, but, when, they become too rarified and obsessive, also enclose the author within a world of her own devising.

In her own brief commentaries on the *Faery Queen*—a work central to Fletcher's study—Woolf, noting the modern distaste for allegory, explains the difference between Spenser's and modern fiction-making in conciliatory terms: "The novelist," she writes, "uses allegory; that is, when he wishes to expound his characters, he makes them think; Spenser impersonated his psychology" [*Collected Essays*, 4, 16]. She then goes on to suggest something very like Fletcher's idea of a macrocosmic-microcosmic diagram:

> In the *Faery Queen* we half consciously have the sense of some pattern hanging in the sky, so that without referring any of the words to a special place, they have that meaning which comes from their being parts of a whole design, and not an isolated fragment of unrelated loveliness. [*Collected Essays*, 4, 15]

Victor de Araujo

The relevance of this statement to "Solid Objects" seems clear. But the paradox and poignancy of the story may reside somewhere between its diagrams and the scheme of the world; partly at least it involves our extra-literary knowledge that the author, despite efforts to find some place in the scheme of things, remained, like her character John, largely an outsider.

"A Haunted House"— The Shattered Glass

*Victor de Araujo**

Midway through "A Haunted House"[1] Virginia Woolf's protagonist remarks: "So fine, so rare, cooly sunk beneath the surface the beam I sought always burnt behind the glass." At the end of the story, in a moment of awareness, she finds the "beam": "Waking, I cry 'Oh, is this *your* buried treasure? The light in the heart.'"

Within this framework of quest and discovery, Virginia Woolf's "A Haunted House" develops its poetic exploration of a series of relationships—between life and death, past and present, senses and imagination, intellect and intuition, hands and heart—utilizing an oblique narrative, which through its emphasis on symbol and suggestion is sometimes difficult to follow. The very compression of the material has led critics to refer to "A Haunted House" as a sketch, "simply a study in impressionism," and "no more a finished work than a painter's preliminary study of a hand or an arm is a finished portrait."[2] The clear-cut desire, however, of a living protagonist to discover the truth held by a dead couple who once had lived in the house—whom she now imaginatively projects wandering as ghosts through rooms—and her attempts to solve the problem, resolved in a final moment of perception, entitle the piece to be considered a short story, in spite of its briefness. Likewise, the variety and range of imagery permit the story an expansion far beyond the immediate events (as clearly as these can be determined through the impressionistic technique of the story) and lead

*Reprinted by permission from *Studies in Short Fiction* 3 (1966):157–64.

from a moment of crisis and awareness to a comment on life that is both fluid and universal.

The story develops within a frame of night, darkness, the power of the unconscious, the puzzle of death. The initial paragraph, beginning, "Whatever hour you woke there was a door shutting," and the next paragraph detailing the comments of the ghostly couple as they supposedly wander about the house are by implication night scenes. Yet in the next two paragraphs, the scene shifts to day, to the life of the outer world, of the senses, the conscious mind. The living are awake, the search is theirs—specifically that of the protagonist—and we are in a world of action. After a transitional paragraph, primarily narrative, in which we learn about the former relationship of the ghosts to each other and to the house, we are immersed in night: outside, the wind and rain with moonbeams splashing and spilling; inside, the steady beam of the lamp. The ghostly couple move and talk; the living couple sleep. The dead discover the sleepers, impart their truth, and the living protagonist wakes to a new awareness. In the end the two worlds become part of one cycle.

Since outer action is for Virginia Woolf less important than inner life—whether that of the conscious or unconscious mind, or that of the emotions—we may grope at times to determine the story's events. The narrative begins: "Whatever hour you woke there was a door shutting. From room to room they went, hand in hand, lifting here, opening there, making sure—a ghostly couple" [*CS*, 116]. Pronouns are our clues to an initial identification of the main characters and their relationships: there are those who wake ("you," presumably the impersonal third person "one") and those who roam (the ghostly couple, "they"). As we proceed—"Here we left it," she said. And he added, "Oh, but here too!" "It's upstairs," she murmured. "And in the garden," he whispered. "Quietly," they said, "or we shall wake them." [*CS*, 116].—the identity of "they" is confirmed, and we are now clear that the "you" of the opening line is more than one person: for the ghosts are concerned with waking "them."

The third paragraph clarifies the identity of "them"; and the focus now shifts from the dead (the ghosts) to the living protagonist, as the scene becomes a daytime one. The relationship has also become closer—between "you" (the dead) and "us" (the living). Furthermore, the pronoun *us* becomes progressively narrowed to the impersonal third person "one," then to *I* and *my*. So, at the end of the passage we are clearly in the viewpoint of some *one* person, who ceases reading to

Victor de Araujo

puzzle over the "spirits" searching through the house, and who attempts to discover the object of their search:

> But it wasn't that you woke us. Oh, no. "They're looking for it; they're drawing the curtain," one might say, and so read on a page or two. "Now they've found it," one would be certain, stopping the pencil on the margin. And then, tired of reading, one might rise and see for oneself, the house all empty, the doors standing open, only the wood pigeons bubbling with content and the hum of the threshing machine sounding from the farm. "What did I come in here for? What did I want to find?" My hands were empty. "Perhaps it's upstairs then?" The apples were in the loft. And so down again, the garden still as ever, only the book had slipped into the grass. [*CS*, 116]

At this point, the problem has shaped itself. The dead are pursuing something in the house; the living, sensitive to a presence, wish to share the discovery. Translating further: one member of a living couple is not disturbed by sight or sound of the ghosts ("it wasn't that you woke us"), but senses the *spiritus loci*, the secret the houses possesses and which she lacks (I arbitrarily say *she* because of the sex of the story's author). The "beam" sought is somewhere and the protagonist must find it. "Silence" and "emptiness" become clues to the relationship of the house to the protagonist. As she leaves the garden and enters the "empty" house, she has not clearly formulated what she is looking for. She sees, however, that her hands are "empty," void of any material treasure. The apples she finds in the loft are presumably not the object of her search, since, by implication, they are still there, and therefore not what the ghostly couple are looking for.

The sounds of wood pigeons and of the threshing machines from the farm contrast with the emptiness of the house, its stillness, and that of the surrounding garden. The outer world is part of the inner dreamlike state; it suggests a mood of late-summer drowsiness, a quiet, peaceful condition approaching sleep, in which the senses record, but seemingly at one remove from the physical.

The completion of the ghosts' search with their assumed discovery is conveyed in the imagery of reflection:

> But they had found it in the drawing-room. Not that one could ever see them. The window panes reflected apples, reflected roses; all the leaves were green in the glass. If they moved in the drawing-

room, the apple only turned its yellow side. Yet, the moment after, if the door was opened, spread about the floor, hung upon the walls, pendant from the ceiling—what? My hands were empty. The shadow of a thrush crossed the carpet; from the deepest wells of silence the wood pigeon drew its bubble of sound. "Safe, safe, safe," the pulse of the house beat softly. "The treasure buried; the room . . . " the pulse stopped short. Oh, was that the buried treasure? [*CS*, 116]

"Death is the glass; death came between us" [*CS*, 116], comments the protagonist at one point in the story. In one sense the life of the spirit, the one the ghosts partake of, reality, is not available to the living seeker. All she can experience, as a substitute, is the reflections in the glass. Her sensory images bounce back from the windowpanes. The light of the sun tricks her and gives nothing but reflected roses and leaves and apples. Standing in the garden, she is unable to see beyond the pane the ghosts moving in the drawing room; she sees nothing but her familiar outer world reflected in the glass. The vision is beautiful, but taken for granted. The movement of the ghosts has as little effect on the outer, physical world, as the apple turning "its yellow side," something that happens naturally when the protagonist changes angles of vision, perhaps, as she walks to the drawing room door. But when she comes in, even the beauty of the outer world has gone; nothing remains. Her hands again "are empty." She sees and hears only the outer world infringe—the shadow of the thrush, the wood pigeon from the farm—at a good distance—breaking the "deepest wells of silence." In the search, however, she is unaware of and denies the reality of this purely reflected life; for, even in shadow, the thrush *breaks* the emptiness of sight; the wood pigeon breaks the emptiness of sound. In the obsession of her search, she records these impressions of peace and harmony and beauty, but they do not fill her present need.

The passage ends with the first statement by the "pulse" or the "heart" of the house: "Safe, safe, safe." This time it beats softly, and the almost inaudible quality is associated with this stage of contemplative unawareness in the protagonist; later, as the story ends, the pulse of the house will beat "wildly," presaging the protagonist's moment of revelation, the moment of communion between the dead embodied in the spirit of place and the living.

The image of *light* is at the core of this story. The protagonist searches for a "beam"; her final discovery is "the light in the heart"

Victor de Araujo

[*CS*, 117]. The light of the sun serves as a barrier, does not penetrate the windowpane, merely reflects the outer world. Likewise, the sun's light gives us the "shadow" of the thrush. Light can both blind and provide illumination, and it seems a matter often of point of view or receptivity in the individual: "A moment later the light had faded. Out in the garden then? But the trees spun darkness for a wandering beam of sun. So fine, so rare, cooly sunk beneath the surface the beam I sought always burnt behind the glass. Death was the glass. . ." [*CS*, 116].

The light that has permitted the shadow of the thrush fades; and in the process, one may suggest, interrupts the full revelation of the pulse of the heart. "Light" here is both the physical light of the sun and the moment of illumination welling up from the unconscious, as an answer to a previous question, "What did I want to find?" The protagonist has forced the mind to give her the answer, and the revelation has been stillborn.

To recapture the light, she returns to the garden; but the sun has gone in, except for a "wandering" beam, and this has been intercepted by the trees. The protagonist contrasts the reflected life she perceives, the light resolving itself either in reflection or shadow (both of which to her are a beam "cooly sunk" *beneath* the surface of life), the world of the senses, of appearances, representing the measure of truth she can grasp in life—with the light she assumes burning "behind the glass," in death.

Typically and briefly, we now learn the identity of the man and woman who once lived in the house and who are now assumed to haunt it:

. . . Death was the glass, death was between us; coming to the woman first, hundreds of years ago, leaving the house, sealing all the windows; the rooms were darkened. He left it, left her, went North, went East, saw the stars turned in the Southern sky; sought the house, found it dropped beneath the Downs. "Safe, safe, safe," the pulse of the house beat gladly. "The Treasure yours." [*CS*, 116–17]

The crux of the problem is stated here in the desire but inability of the living to bridge the barriers of the past, of death. Similarly, the death of the woman, one assumes, isolated her from her loved one and the house. "He left it, left her, went North." Later, dead himself, he returns to the house. Communication is reëstablished. "Safe, safe, safe," the pulse of the house beat gladly. "The Treasure, yours." This return reëstablishes communion between the man, his wife, and the house, which had witnessed their happiness. The material world of the house and its surroundings becomes transmuted into an eternal spirit because of its associations for the dead who there found joy. It has become, in a sense, immortalized.

At this point, the scene shifts abruptly from day to night; from daytime quietness and peace in the garden and the house to nightime wind and rain in the avenue of trees outside (but calm in the steadiness of lamp and candle inside):

> The wind roars up the avenue. Trees stoop and bend this way and that. Moonbeams splash and spill wildly in the rain. But the beam of the lamp falls straight from the window. The candle burns stiff and still. Wandering through the house, opening the windows, whispering not to wake us, the ghostly couple seek their joy. [*CS*, 117]

Daytime is the time of the sun, of the outer physical world, the world of the living who wish to perceive beyond the veil of matter but cannot do so. Nighttime is the time of the moon, the imagination, the spirit, intuition, insight—not the senses. And it is at night that the dead, holders of the truth, roam and impart their knowledge. The "joy" of the ghosts is in the house and around it. It is also, ultimately, the joy of the living. The dead and the living live through each other; since time is annihilated in eternal values, in truth.

> "Here we slept," she says. And he adds, "Kisses without number." "Waking in the morning—" "Silver between the trees." "Upstairs—" "In the garden—" "When summer came—" "In winter snowtime—" The doors go shutting far in the distance, gently knocking like the pulse of a heart. [*CS*, 117]

As the ghosts approach—"Nearer they come; cease at the doorway"—the living couple are about to fall asleep. Symbolically, because of the glass between them, for the dead to approach, the living must at least be in a state of simulated death—sleep; since in both sleep and death the unconscious of man is freed of time and space. Here, the moment of passivity begins, in which the vision will be imparted. In the daytime the active search prevented it. Always the vision escaped.

Apparently, we have here an allegory of the creative imagination. Man's conscious search for a vision, awareness, is often frustrated. He probes, he imagines; but the answer to his question often does not come. Yet the unconscious, in sleep, often provides the moment of insight; provides the answer to the mathematician's problem, to the writer's dilemma. Characters, scene, plot gel; and through these constituents of fiction, suddenly, the moment of truth is revealed:

> Nearer they come; cease at the doorway. The wind falls, the rain slides silver down the glass. Our eyes darken; we hear no steps beside us; we see no lady spread her ghostly cloak. His hands shield the lantern. "Look," he breathes. "Sound asleep. Love upon their lips." [*CS*, 117]

The rain, transformed by the light of the moon, "slides silver down the glass." But the illumined rain is still outside, on the other side of the glass. The light of the lantern, likewise, is "shielded" by the ghost's hands. The barrier between dead and living, past and present, spirit and flesh, imagination and senses yet remains.

Now everything, however, is bathed in silver and moonlight. The world of the living has ceased to exist; and in the unconscious state of sleep the present tenants will be able to perceive the ghosts:

> Stooping, holding their silver lamp above us, long they look and deeply. Long they pause. The wind drives straightly; the flame stoops slightly. Wild beams of moonlight cross both the floor and wall, and meeting, stain the faces bent; the faces pondering; the faces that search the sleepers and seek their hidden joy. [*CS*, 117]

Deliberately or not, the pronoun *their* is ambiguous. Although the "hidden joy" is presumably that of the present tenants, it may also be that of the ghostly couple. The ambiguity is fitting because the story works to a point of communion of living and dead, a communication in terms of time—present and past being part of one flux, one continuum.

The rhetoric of the passage, in its deliberate rhythm, its balanced pattern, effectively shows the pace before the final revelation. The beams of moonlight cross the glass, come indoors. This is the hour of the past, of the dead; they even assume identity, "faces" stained, pondering, searching. They hold the life-giving lamp, a "silver," not golden lamp, ironically one of reflected light. As a result, "Safe, safe, safe," the heart of the house beats proudly. For temporarily the house belongs to none but the dead. And the final relationship between the couple and their world of happy memories is reëchoed: "'Long years'—he sighs. 'Again you found me.' 'Here,' she murmurs, 'sleeping; in the garden reading; laughing, rolling apples in the loft. Here we left our treasure—'"

The recollections echo the present life in the house—the moments of seeing, listening, reading, sleeping—the moments of vision that exist in the quotidian; moments of awareness that occur—as Mabel Waring remarks in Virginia Woolf's "The New Dress"[3]—when less expected; perfect moments—at the seaside, carving the mutton, opening a letter. The happiness the ghosts recall has become the spirit of the place and now haunts the present tenants, in particular the protagonist herself, because many of the sources of joy are still the same. Communication between the two dead has been fully reëstablished as they revisit the place of their former love and happiness; now the "light" of their silver lamp brings the answer to the sleeping protagonist: "Stooping, their light lifts the lids upon my eyes. 'Safe! safe! safe!' the pulse of the house beats wildly. Waking, I cry 'Oh, is this *your* buried treasure? The light in the heart'" [*CS*, 117].

The light that "lifts the lids" is of course both physical light and "insight." Previously, the eyes of the protagonist had "darkened." Now they are illuminated. She is still unable to "see" the ghostly couple; but the meaning of the "beam" becomes clear. Although she had sought some secret that she could hold in her "hands," the buried treasure is none but the "light in the heart," happiness, love, each man's transmutation of the world around him through his sense of beauty and imagination; and she and her loved one have "love upon their lips."

The ending is ironic. We are blind to what we have ourselves, and seek it instead in others. The dead have the answer, the protagonist believes; the past must illumine the present. It does; but only in suggesting continuity in life, sameness of human experience and human relationships, fluidity in time.

"A Haunted House" also suggests that the beam that illuminates must shine on the physical life, the life of the senses. Happiness comes from apples rolled and books read and wood pigeons bubbling; a sharing of what one experiences, the beauty one absorbs. And love, when the lovers are disembodied, becomes part of the *spiritus loci*—in this

Frank Baldanza

instance a house and surroundings where it has been shared. This then is the link between past and present, and will be the link to the future.

Mortality and eternity, Virginia Woolf seems to suggest in this story, are one flux. The unconscious reveals the link between life and death; truth is a matter of intuition and feeling, not to be fully apprehended by intellect and logic. The conscious search, the will in action can provide only an uncomfortable sense of something missed, some graspable object or "beam" which constantly eludes. Man's consciousness at rest, however, dulled in sleep, passive, frees the unconscious to full receptivity. And the result is a revelation of shattered glass—life and death as one fluid continuum of time and space, with memory and imagination as the links.

Notes

1. Virginia Woolf, *Collected Shorter Fiction*, pp. 116–17. This story has been reprinted, among other places, in *Masters and Masterpieces of the Short Story*, Second Series, Joshua McClennen, ed. (New York, 1960), pp. 561–562.

2. David Daiches, *Virginia Woolf* (Norfolk, Conn., 1942), p. 44.

3. Woolf, *Collected Shorter Fiction*, pp. 164–171. Moments of insight and perfect happiness occur also to Mrs. Ramsay and Lily Briscoe in Virginia Woolf's well-known novel *To The Lighthouse*. In fact, the novel ends with Lily's unexpected moment of vision, a glimpse of reality that enables her to complete her painting.

Clarissa Dalloway's "Party Consciousness"
Frank Baldanza*

Richard and Clarissa Dalloway have a prolonged fictional life outside of the novel to which they give their name: they first show up unexpectedly aboard the *Euphrosyne* in *The Voyage Out*, Virginia Woolf's first novel. Here Clarissa's furs and jewels, the Dalloways' social position,

*Reprinted by permission from *Modern Fiction Studies* 1 (1956):24–30.© 1956 Purdue University Research Foundation.

and Richard's obvious success in life at first create opposition and antagonism on the part of the middle-class passengers; but by the time
they leave the ship, the Dalloways have charmed nearly everyone on
board. They are also the basis of a group of short stories, "The New
Dress," "Together and Apart," "A Summing Up," and "The Man Who
Loved His Kind," only the first of which was published during Mrs.
Woolf's lifetime. The Dalloways serve in these stories as party-givers,
a pretext for bringing together groups of people whose encounters, joy-
ous, boring, or hateful, are the substance of the respective works of art
in which they appear.

   In their total significance, Richard and Clarissa Dalloway have a
symbolic value for Mrs. Woolf: they embody the average traits of people on the social, cultural, and economic level with which she was most
familiar. To be sure, Clarissa herself is the least educated and least
literate of the characters to whom Mrs. Woolf had given a major status
at the time she wrote *Mrs. Dalloway,* her fourth novel; but this was
certainly a conscious choice, since it left Mrs. Dalloway free from the
complications of other people's theories and ideas about life. Mrs.
Woolf's intention is clear in Clarissa's speech from *The Voyage Out:*

> I always think it's living, not dying, that counts. I really respect
> some snuffy old stockbroker who's gone on adding up column after
> column all his days, and trotting back to his villa at Brixton with
> some old pug dog he worships, and a dreary little wife sitting at the
> end of the table, and going off to Margate for a fortnight—I assure
> you I know heaps like that—well, they seem to me *really* nobler than
> poets whom everyone worships, just because they are geniuses and
> die young. (London, 1929, p. 58)

Mrs. Woolf puts the same thing more succinctly in her diary: "More
and more do I repeat my own version of Montaigne—'It's life that
matters'" (London, 1953, p. 72).

   The focus of reality as the Dalloways represent it is the party. Clarissa, in a memorable passage from *Mrs. Dalloway,* smarts at the im-
putations of her husband (who says parties are bad for her heart) and
of Peter Walsh (who says she gives parties for snobbish reasons):

> And both of them were quite wrong. What she liked was simply
> life. "That's what I do it for," she said, speaking aloud, to life. . . .
> But to go deeper, beneath what people said . . . in her own mind
> now, what did it mean to her, this thing called life? Oh, it was very

queer. Here was So-and-so in South Kensington; someone else up in Bayswater; and somebody else, say, in Mayfair. And she felt quite continuously a sense of their existence; and she felt what a waste; and she felt what a pity; and she felt if only they could be brought together; so she did it, and it was an offering; to combine, to create; but to whom?

An offering for the sake of offering, perhaps. Anyhow, it was her gift. (London, 1933, pp. 183–184)

And this complex gift is the result of a simpler and more basic one, presented early in the book: "Her only gift was knowing people almost by instinct, she thought, walking on. If you put her in a room with someone, up went her back like a cat's; or she purred" (p. 15).

Mrs. Woolf here indulges one of the deepest instincts of her nature: in her diary when she discusses the various assortments of consciousnesses which go to make up any one person, she singles out "the party consciousness" and "the frock consciousness" as examples of two of these which she used to portray character:

. . . People secrete an envelope which connects them and protects them from others, like myself, who am outside the envelope, foreign bodies. These states are very difficult (obviously I grope for words) but I'm always coming back to it. . . . You must not break it. It is something real. You must keep it up—conspire together. Still I cannot get at what I mean. (p. 75)

In the short stories Mrs. Woolf tried to get at what she meant artistically, as she was not able to do in her diary. "The New Dress," for example, is a study of the "frock consciousness" gone wrong. Mabel Waring is tortured throughout a Dalloway party by a consciousness that her new yellow frock is dowdy and dated, and she looks like a fly in a saucer of milk. "For a party makes things either much more real, or much less real, she thought . . . " [*CS*, 166]. The identical thought comes to Clarissa at the climax of her party in *Mrs. Dalloway:* "Every time she gave a party she had this feeling of being something not herself, and that every one was unreal in some way; much more real in another" (p. 257). This state of intensified reality within a context of unreality, which comes to Lily Briscoe in *To the Lighthouse* just before her final ecstatic vision, is a mystic commonplace for the expression of a heightened consciousness, as with the Magi of Eliot's poem who cannot decide whether they have seen a birth or a death. The envelope is an extension of one's consciousness for the dual purpose of protection and of communication. In the case of Mabel Waring, her intense feeling of self-loathing and shame needs a protective envelope. Within this chrysalis, she experiences an acute suspension between two or three different emotions, a state of mind that inevitably accompanies the heightened awareness of these periods. She remembers the moments of ecstasy which occurred as she planned the dress, as she was kind to the dressmaker during the fittings, and the like; and the harrowing contrast with the present is only relieved by her vision of future moments—she will read a book by an American or go to hear a miner describe life in the pits, and her life will revive.

In "Together and Apart," on the other hand, we have a study of a successful encounter at a party where the aura projected by the individuals serves as a means of communication. In this case, Clarissa introduces Ruth Anning and Roderick Searle, virtual strangers. Their fragmentary conversation only serves to interrupt the internal reverie which their encounter inspires; each reviews his whole life, the disappointments and failures and slackening of forces that come with age. Against this melancholy realization is juxtaposed, in another of these suspensions between several different emotions, a moment of blinding love in which both persons rise to a height of rare ecstasy when Ruth crystallizes their common interests by remarking "I love Canterbury."

> . . . now, quite suddenly, like a white bolt in a mist . . . there it happened; the old ecstasy of life; its invincible assault; for it was unpleasant, at the same time that it rejoiced and rejuvenated and filled the veins and nerves with threads of ice and fire; it was terrifying. "Canterbury twenty years ago," said Miss Anning, as one lays a shade over an intense light, or covers some burning peach with a green leaf, for it is too strong, too ripe, too full. [CS, 186–87]

"A Summing Up" consists simply of a paean of ecstatic praise for Mrs. Dalloway on the part of Sasha Latham, who feels that a Dalloway party, and the human relations it inspires, is "'the supreme achievement of the human race'" [CS, 203]. The suspension in this very short piece is between Sasha's consciousness of this achievement and the contrast presented by the primeval, ugly, brutal world just over the Dalloway garden wall; the climax of the story occurs as Sasha peeks over the wall just as her companion suggests they go back to the house.

Frank Baldanza

On the evening of June 26, 1925, Virginia Woolf attended a garden party given by Roger Fry; a "chilly windy night" may have contributed to the revulsion against the "party consciousness" which she recorded in her diary the next day:

> And I do not love my kind, I detest them. I pass them by. I let them break on me like dirty rain drops. No longer can I summon up that energy which, when it sees one of these dry little shapes floating past, or rather stuck on the rock, sweeps round them, steeps them, infuses them, nerves them, and so finally fills them and creates them. Once I had a gift for doing this, and a passion, and it made parties arduous and exciting. (*CS*, 79)

The opening sentence of this passage was one that haunted Mrs. Woolf: in one form it is the title of a story we shall analyze directly; in other forms it recurs in *To the Lighthouse* and *The Years*. The phrase is always used ironically for the kind of person—invariably a man—who prides himself on love of his kind but who is fundamentally incapable of demonstrating such love. In "The Man Who Loved His Kind," Prickett Ellis is invited to a party by Richard Dalloway, and when he arrives is introduced to Miss O'Keefe. This introduction of two people is, of course, the central function of the party; but in this case Ellis consciously acts out to violate the terms on which the party consciousness is maintained. He is angered and hurt at the Dalloway display of wealth and at the childish inconsequence of the way of life which it represents, as were the passengers on the *Euphrosyne*. Miss O'Keefe, who was earlier wounded at the sight of a woman and children peering over the fence at the party, tries valiantly to "conspire" with him, but the clash of feelings that Ellis foments completely dissipates her "envelope" and the story ends thus:

> "I am afraid I am one of those very ordinary people," he said, getting up, "who love their kind."
> Upon which Miss O'Keefe almost shouted: "So do I."
> Hating each other, hating the whole houseful of people who had given them this painful, this disillusioning evening, these two lovers of their kind got up, and without a word, parted forever. [*CS*, 194]

The complexity of the story is heightened by the relative sympathy with which Ellis's point of view is represented; throughout his encounter with Miss O'Keefe, he remembers a poor family that had given him a clock because he had won a legal case for them; we see the contrast in his mind between the way he helps the poor and the way the Dalloways live, but we see how tawdry his existence is at the same time.

The novel *Mrs. Dalloway* is directly related to these stories, since in one sense it *is* the story of a party: as the book opens, Mrs. Dalloway steps out of her door, on the way to buy flowers for her party. And insistently throughout the day represented in the book "remember my party" chimes in as a major *leitmotif:* in the morning Clarissa invites Peter, somewhat ironically, and he muses on her parties at various times during the day; Richard reminds Lady Bruton and Hugh Whitbread of the party at luncheon; Sir William Bradshaw, who is late because of the suicide of Septimus Warren Smith, connects the two major strands of the book (the Dalloways and the Smiths) in his presence at the party.

Further, Mrs. Woolf's diary reveals that some portions of the book are drawn from her own party-going experiences. In June of 1923, for example, Mrs. Woolf describes a week-end she spent at Garsington, the home of Lady Ottoline Morrell. She determines to bring into *Mrs. Dalloway* "the despicableness of people like Ott." From the description that follows, we can see that Mrs. Dalloway's inviting Ellis Henderson is based on Lady Ottoline's courting of "a black shabby embroideress": "That's one of her horrors—she's always being kind in order to say to herself at night, then Ottoline invites the poor little embroideress to her party and so to round off her own picture of herself" (pp. 55–56).

We saw that Clarissa defines life as bringing together people from South Kensington and Bayswater with people from Mayfair; but this is only half a definition. Earlier in the day, standing at a window, she has seen the little old lady across the street mount the stairs and putter about her room. Clarissa has been meditating on how odious were the effects of love and religion on people she cared for: Peter Walsh is made ridiculous by the frumps for whom he ruined himself; her daughter is corrupted by her hatefully shabby religious tutor, Miss Kilman. Suddenly in a moment of intense recognition Clarissa sees that the old lady opposite has a magnificence in the whole problem:

> . . . that's the miracle, that's the mystery; that old lady, she meant, whom she could see going from chest of drawers to dressing table. She could still see her. And the supreme mystery which Kilman

might say she had solved, or Peter might say he had solved, but Clarissa didn't believe either of them had the ghost of an idea of solving, was simply this: here was one room; there another. Did religion solve that, or love? (pp. 192–193)

Thus the little old lady puttering in her room represents the isolation of the soul which, to Clarissa's mind, neither love nor religion can eliminate: it is perhaps the essence of the Bloomsbury point of view that a party should succeed where love and religion do not.

As the party begins, Clarissa has serious doubts of its success, but once it is launched, she is convinced it will go well. A short time later Sir William and Lady Bradshaw arrive with the news that Septimus Warren Smith, a shell-shocked veteran, has committed suicide late in the afternoon. Clarissa has never heard of him before (although the reader has followed Septimus' stream of consciousness regularly throughout the book); but she has a curious sympathy with the young man, based partially on her own dislike of Bradshaw and her perception of his part in Septimus' death. Strangely moved, she leaves the party and stands alone in the little room; again she sees the little old lady opposite, preparing for bed. But this time the reader sees an added significance in the old lady, because when Septimus jumped out of the window on the approach of Dr. Bradshaw, he had just seen a little old man descend the stairs opposite—a parallel which John Hawley Roberts was the first to point out. In another of her moments of vision, Clarissa deeply and wholeheartedly sanctions the young stranger's attitude.

Septimus was mad, and throughout the book Mrs. Woolf has presented his experience sympathetically and ingenuously for what it was. This very special exercise in point of view—giving a serious representation of how birds in the trees sing in Greek and how voices transmit messages of urgent intensity—is calculated to stress the prime characteristic of madness, which is failure to communicate. That is the meaning, too, of the little old man and the old lady—"here one room; there another," as Clarissa said. Septimus' isolation is entire: when the ghost of Evans, his dead officer, appears to him no one else sees it; the message which he insists that his wife copy down for him means nothing to her. There is no one in the world who shares Septimus' view of reality, and yet to him, the flames that lick about his sofa from time to time are intensely painful, regardless of what his wife and the doctors say. His form of madness is simply loneliness intensified beyond the point of human endurance. Clarissa sees this:

> A thing there was that mattered; a thing, wreathed about with chatter, defaced, obscured, in her own life, let drop every day in corruption, lies, chatter. This he had preserved. Death was defiance. Death was an attempt to communicate, people feeling the impossibility of reaching the center which, mystically, evaded them; closeness drew apart; rapture faded; one was alone. There was an embrace in death. (pp. 277–278)

Thus Mrs. Woolf presents the two poles of existence as she sees it: Clarissa and Septimus, parties and suicides, communcation and death. But like the poles, these two aspects of experience are both part of a continuous globe of consciousness that involves everyone. The resolution of this polar separation in the terms of experience is to be found in Mrs. Woolf's Whitman-like mysticism. Clarissa very early in the book consoles herself at the thought of death by the assurance that she is part of the places and people she has loved—"being laid between the people she knew best, who lifted her on their branches, as she had seen the trees lift the mist . . . " (p. 16). Later in the novel, Peter gives us a view of Clarissa on the Shaftesbury Avenue bus which is remarkably like Whitman on the Brooklyn Ferry:

> It was unsatisfactory, they agreed, how little one knew people. But she said, sitting on the bus going up Shaftesbury Avenue, she felt herself everywhere; not "here, here, here"; and she tapped the back of the seat; but everywhere. She waved her hand, going up Shaftesbury Avenue. She was all that. So that to know her, or any one, one must seek out the people who completed them; even the places. Odd affinities she had with people she had never spoken to, some woman in the street, some man behind a counter—even trees, or barns. It ended in a transcendental theory which, with her horror of death, allowed her to believe, or say that she believed (for all her scepticism), that since our apparitions, the part of us which appears, are so momentary compared with the other, the unseen part of us, which spreads wide, the unseen might survive, be recovered somehow attached to this person or that, or even haunting certain places, after death. Perhaps—perhaps. (pp. 229–230)

Obviously, Mrs. Woolf somehow equates parties with life, and although the examples of F. Scott Fitzgerald and Proust might lend support to the artistic feasibility of the idea, there is more to it than that. Bloomsbury had deep roots in Cambridge, and both the constitution and preoccupations of the group were determined by the friendships and enthusiasms of the male members in their college days. By all accounts, and particularly in the books of Clive Bell and the second of the *Two Memoirs* of Lord Keynes, we have a full explanation of the overwhelming influence of the philosophy of G. E. Moore on the youthful members of the group. Although we can hardly pause here even to nod at the complexities of this influence, we can see briefly that the heart of G. E. Moore's doctrine as Bloomsbury saw it was that "By far the most valuable things, which we know or can imagine, are certain states of consciousness, which may be roughly described as the pleasures of human intercourse and the enjoyment of beautiful objects." The conciseness of the statement is directly related to the intensity with which the group took it up as a manifesto. Nearly all reality, in their thought, ends in "states of mind," and when other considerations—even when a chapter of Moore's *Principia Ethica*—stood in the way of hypostasizing the state of mind as the absolute value, out it went. They had sufficient reason even in Moore himself, for supposing that "it is only for the sake of these things . . . that anyone can be justified in performing any public or private duty; that they are the *raison d'être* of virtue; that it is they . . . that form the rational ultimate end of human action and the sole criterion of social progress . . . " Of course the passion with which the group adopted these values reflects the depth of their commitment to all the assumptions of English aestheticism as concentrated in Pater and Wilde.

The subjects of Bloomsbury conversation as Keynes presents them tally remarkably with many of Mrs. Woolf's basic concerns in epistemology. But if Mrs. Woolf concerned herself with the same basic preoccupations as this group of male friends, she substituted the standard of sensibility for their scientific mensuration, and she projected such questions directly into the flux of consciousness while she presented them as occurring in the course of average lives of the kind of people she knew. The moment of vision in her novels is a flowering of a good state of mind in the consciousness. Jacob Flanders is a mosaic of the states of mind of others; and *Mrs. Dalloway* is composed of an interrelated series of states of mind; even those of a madman, presented as absolutes in themselves, without condemnation, sentimentality, or excuses. The absence of violent action in her novels, aside from the suicide of Septimus, is obviously a part of the doctrine of the irrelevance of action to good states of mind. Her refusal to accept the pat solution and the two-and-thirty chapters of ordinary novel structure is a protest against the kind of reality such structure reflects. The troubled, unresolved, and often painful tone of scene after scene in her novels comes from regarding unflinchingly all the components of a state of mind. Many of these states become standardized in her novels: there are the "party consciousness," the "who am I? where am I?" state, the "riding an omnibus" state, the "I am a tree" state, the "it is finished" state, and the state of mystical exaltation in solitude in which the emotions become a liquid flood, a sharp point, or a dark wedge. Mrs. Woolf's unwavering honesty and directness of attack are the aesthetic corollary of the scientific rigor of the men in the group, and she knows that this is the case: "But I recognise my own limitation; not a good ratiocinator, Lytton used to say. Do I instinctively keep my mind from analyzing, which would impair creativeness?" The answer is pretty obviously yes. Mrs. Woolf always had a hearty feeling for original sin and could never have shared the faith of the others in the sweet reasonableness of human beings. She was too acutely aware, from her own suffering, of the irrational and insane springs within man. Aside from her husband's statement that she committed suicide in fear of a return of a nervous malady, there is ample evidence in the diary of faintings, excruciating headaches, pains like those of childbirth, and the like, all of which show that Mrs. Woolf herself was profoundly aware of the precariousness of human reason.

Both of these aspects of her experience—the value system of G. E. Moore, and her own experience with nervous derangement—are the basis of *Mrs. Dalloway*.

Already in this book one sees a strong influence by Proust making itself felt; at least in part the theory of "caves" of past time hollowed out behind her characters, to which Mrs. Woolf devotes several pages of triumphant description in her diary, must come from that source. But as she progresses, we find the Dalloway "party consciousness" continuing as a kind of concrete vestige in the later novels—in the experience of Jinny in *The Waves* or of Delia in *The Years*, for example— while the "state of mind" swells into the symphonic elaborations of the dinner in *To the Lighthouse*, the oversoul of the six characters in *The Waves*, and the pageant in *Between the Acts*.

James Hafley

On One of Virginia Woolf's Short Stories

James Hafley*

I do not suppose that very many people have read Virginia Woolf's short stories with anything like the attention that is given to her novels. "Kew Gardens" and "The Mark on the Wall," which are called short stories mainly because we now conceive of the essay merely as a form for the objective communication of verifiable truths, are familiar at least in part, since they have been quoted from to illustrate things about the novels; "The New Dress," among the short stories proper, seems to be the anthologists' favorite, and is therefore perhaps the best-known of them. The point is that you can still surprise people by telling them to read "The Duchess and the Jeweller" or "Lappin and Lapinova": the fact that Virginia Woolf, of all people, wrote something with a "plot" comes rather as a shock. And however well you may know the stories you can constantly surprise yourself by re-readings of, say, "The Shooting Party" or "Solid Objects" or "Moments of Being": it is in this instance the shock that always attends the contemplation of perfection or near-perfection.

I should like to hold up for brief consideration here the story called "Moments of Being." It is primarily worth looking at simply for itself, as a beautifully accomplished art-work; but it is also valuable in so far as it offers a microcosmic illustration of some of Virginia Woolf's techniques in the novels, as well as the other short stories. It was first published in *Échanges*, for December, 1929, under its original title, now its sub-title, "Slater's Pins Have No Points"; and subsequently included in *A Haunted House* (1943). And I have chosen to write about it rather than one of the other stories for no better reason than that it happens to be my faviorite among them.

The situation in "Moments of Being" is, or seems at first, quite simple: Fanny Wilmot, a young music student, has been listening to her teacher, Julia Craye, perform a Bach fugue; Fanny's corsage has fallen from her dress, and as she looks about on the floor for the pin with which it has been fastened, she creates for herself the story of Miss Craye's life, having been started upon this imaginative performance by Miss Craye's sympathetic remark that "Slater's pins have no

*Reprinted by permission from *Modern Fiction Studies* 2 (1956): 13–16. © 1956 Purdue University Research Foundation.

points—don't you always find that?" The "action" of the short story—what it imitates—is not at all the past life of Julia Craye, but the mind of Fanny Wilmot engaged in the composition of that life; and so the story is about Fanny, who in a matter of seconds brings together all the wisps of information and pseudo-information that she has ever heard about her teacher and synthesizes them, in the light of the remark about pins, into what is for her a pattern just as complete and revelatory as the Bach fugue to which she has been listening; and the form of her composition takes, quite appropriately, the form of a fugue, as the theme—"Slater's pins have no points"—is stated and developed by one voice after another, the entrance of each new voice being indicated by a shift in time sequence, and is then given its comprehensive resolution. The story begins with the theme, stated by Julia; when Fanny Wilmot has partially developed this theme, she states it herself, but assumes Julia's voice to do so—that is, she puts inverted commas around the phrase. After some additional development, the theme is again stated, this time in Fanny's own voice; and she goes on to complete the development. The theme appears a fourth time at the end of the story, after Fanny has realized all of the possibilities that it suggested to her and has resolved it. But it is stated here by Julia again: the end of Fanny's fugue becomes the opening measure of any other person's—of the reader's, for example—just as the last chord of the Bach fugue played by Julia had coincided with the first measure of Fanny's, spoken by her.

Fanny's mind works largely with images; it is to her amazing that a woman like Julia Craye—poised, serene, self-contained with her art—should know anything about pins: about the world in which pins are bought and used and judged. For Miss Craye lives in the "cool glassy world of Bach fugues" [CS, 209], just as her twin brother Julius, now dead, had lived as an archaeologist in a world of "Roman glasses" [CS, 209]. Surely Miss Craye must be conscious of "the pane of glass" [CS, 210] which separates her world from *the* world, separates herself as it separated Julius from ordinary people; all that she really has is a "glassy surface" [CS, 210] to see. Her favorite flowers are crocuses, those "glossy bright flowers" [CS, 213], and she can be pictured counting out some of her meager supply of money to purchase not pins but "an old mirror" [CS, 214].

Miss Craye has never married, and it is natural that to a young girl like Fanny Wilmot this would be the most persistent fact, the one responsible for whatever directions her story will take. (Ironically, Julia's remark about the pins has actually "transfixed" Fanny, who nevertheless thinks, "What need had [Julia] of pins? For she was not so much dressed as cased, like a beetle compactly in its sheath, blue in winter, green in summer" [*CS*, 209].) Fanny does not think of Julia directly as a spinster, but, more kindly, as living in a world apart from the *real* one, having on her face a look that seems to say

> "Stars, sun, moon . . . the daisy in the grass, fires, frost on the window pane, my heart goes out to you. But," it always seemed to add, "you break, you pass, you go." And simultaneously it covered both these states of mind with "I can't reach you—I can't get at you."
> [*CS*, 210]

And Fanny reasons that it is to break such a spell that Julia has attempted familiarity with the everyday world of Slater's pins. Fanny seems torn between a regret that Julia should so lower herself and a fear that perhaps the real world, which *is* mutable and transitory, may not withstand the sudden entrance of this woman whose own life seems to embody a permanence and certainty that "life itself" cannot manage. She must at once defend Miss Craye and defend the world; she does so, of course, and quite without realizing it, by melding the two in the fluid permanence of her meditation.

On another level, then, the short story itself achieves the same synthesis of opposites as an art-work. This paradoxical unity is most succinctly imaged by the description of Julia at the end of the story: "Out of the night she burnt like a dead white star" [*CS*, 214]. The ingenious ambiguity there—whether "dead" is to be taken as qualifying "white" or "star," that is to say—offers a syntactical equivalent of the overall ambiguity. For if Julia has finally gone beyond the pane of glass that separated her from the stars, has finally become the star she looked at through a glass darkly, there is also the meaning that by reaching out for life itself, in the very act of breaking down the barrier and entering the real world, she has lost her own life. Again, "out of the night" may be read either as "in the otherwise dark world" or as "from the night in which the other stars still shone"; for there is a suggestion that if Julia has lost her own life she has also destroyed the "real world" which—as Fanny would have it, and we must remember that it is Fanny's consciousness rather than Julia's which these ambiguities define—

she had been so eager to possess. (The fact that I am not trying to "do an Empson" here will I think become clear if it is noticed that the problem and techniques involved in this story are present in every one of Virginia Woolf's novels as well.)

But this situation is given its final dimension by another word in the short story: when Fanny has completed her story of Julia Craye's past life, and has found the pin, she looks up and discovers Julia seated before the window "in a moment of ecstasy" [*CS*, 214], holding a flower in her hands; but now, Fanny thinks, she really *sees* Julia—now that she has evidently realized the other woman's life. She knows now that Julia remained unmarried through fear of entering into the uncertainties, the flux, of "reality," preferring to remain in the secure world that was defined, stabilized, and immobilized for her by her music and her brother's archaeological specimens; preferring to remember vividly how lovely Kensington had been in the days when "it was like a village" [*CS*, 211], and to criticize the modern life, "to denounce acridly the draughts in the Tubes" [*CS*, 211]. And as for men, naturally Julia preferred to believe that their only use was, surely, to protect women. It is a moment of triumph for Fanny, then, the moment in which suddenly she "understands" Julia Craye, believes her to be happy in her own way, after all, and can divorce herself from the music teacher without compunction or rancor. And there follows this remarkable passage:

> All seemed transparent, for a moment, to the gaze of Fanny Wilmot, as if looking through Miss Craye, she saw the very fountain of her being spurting its pure silver drops. She saw back and back into the past behind her. . . . She saw Julia—— [*CS*, 214]

The key word, the *real* revelation—by which I mean that which is given to the reader of the story, as distinct from the revelation apparently given to Fanny—is of course that one innocent adjective, *transparent*. Fanny is now "looking through" Julia, and all *seems* transparent for her, whereas all *is* transparent for the reader: by developing this fugue on the theme of Slater's pins, Fanny has put herself, though she does not realize it during the course of the story, precisely into Julia Craye's situation as she had first imagined it. It is now *she* who observes a glassy surface, who has entered a cool glassy world of her own making and stands behind a pane of glass that separates her from reality.

Julia Craye is seated before the window, just as her brother's Roman vase had stood in the window and been jealously guarded from possible danger when a child entered the house; Julia now stands in the same relation to Fanny as the vase did to Julius, and as the music does to Julia herself. For Fanny, too, this is a "moment of ecstasy" [*CS*, 214], and the story concludes as she "pinned the flower to her breast with trembling fingers" [*CS*, 214], transfixing it as she had been transfixed. Julia, so Fanny imagines, can think after one of her rare trips alone to Hampton Court to see the flowers that

> it was a victory. It was something that lasted; something that mattered for ever. She strung the afternoon on the necklace of memorable days, which was not too long for her to be able to recall this one or that one; this view, that city; to finger it, to feel it, to savour, sighing, the quality that made it unique. [*CS*, 213]

Yet, Fanny goes on to think, "one pitied her for always doing everything alone" [*CS*, 213]. But so it is with this moment, the moment of this short story while Fanny searches for the pointless pin of reality and at the same time creates, herself, what she believes to be the "real" meaning of Julia Craye. That meaning depends for its life upon its isolation, its separation from life itself by the pane of glass upon whose surface it is seen—or, for either way will do, the mirror in which it is a reflection of Fanny herself. Thus, when "Julia opened her arms. Julia kissed her on the lips," Fanny can believe that "Julia possessed it"— reality. She has imagined Julia as grasping, clutching at life as she clutched at the flower in her hands; "but she did not possess it, enjoy it, not entirely and altogether" [*CS*, 211]. And again, following the abortive love scene on the Serpentine—one that exists, of course, only in Fanny's consciousness—she has imagined Julia's thinking, "I can't have it, I can't possess it" [*CS*, 212]. But now Fanny's apparent realization of Julia seems also to be Julia's realization of the goal that Fanny has created for her; so, "Julia opened her arms" [*CS*, 214] recalls the love scene; and, from Fanny's isolated point of view, "Julia possessed it." The nature of Julia's ecstatic moment we do not know; the nature of Fanny's we do; they are both of them, in Hardy's phrase which gives the story its title, "moments of being." And the final question, of course, is the meaning of this "being" which exists so precariously, so privately, so preposterously in its false truth. But that is a question which the author need not, should not, answer; and the reader, if he

The Critics

tries to answer it, can only follow along exactly the same path that Fanny Wilmot started down when she lost her pin and bent to look for it.

What you have got to do, Virginia Woolf says with her short stories and her novels, is settle for the ambiguity, the pin and the rose, reality and the pane of glass; for it is, finally, only the ambiguity which is clear-cut and only the paradox which allows the moment of being. Fanny Wilmot's truth is pointedly false; it has led her perhaps away from reality and certainly to a moment of complete self-deception; but, on the other hand, Slater's pins have no points.

> The idea has come to me that what I want now to do is to saturate every atom. I mean to eliminate all waste, deadness, superfluity: to give the moment whole; whatever it includes. Say that the moment is a combination of thought; sensation; the voice of the sea. Waste, deadness, come from the inclusion of things that don't belong to the moment; this appalling narrative business of the realist: getting on from lunch to dinner: it is false, unreal, merely conventional. Why admit anything to literature that is not poetry—by which I mean saturated.
>
> —*A Writer's Diary* (1954), p. 136

144

Chronology

1878   Leslie Stephen marries Julia Duckworth in March.

1879   Vanessa Stephen born in May.

1880   Julian Thoby Stephen born in September.

1882   Virginia Stephen born in January.

1883   Adrian Stephen born in October.

1895   Virginia's mother, Julia Stephen, dies in April.

1895   Virginia's first mental breakdown in May.

1897   Virginia begins her diary in January.
        Thoby Stephen enters Cambridge University in October.

1904   Virginia's father, Leslie Stephen, dies in February.
        Virginia's second mental breakdown in May.
        Virginia publishes unsigned review in the *Guardian* in December.

1905   Virginia pronounced cured in January.

1906   Virginia writes her first short stories: "Phyllis and Rosamond," "The Mysterious Case of Miss V.," "Journal of Mistress Joan Martyn."
        Virginia's brother, Thoby Stephen, dies of typhoid fever in November.

1907   Vanessa Stephen marries Clive Bell in February.
        Virginia and Adrian set up house at 29 Fitzroy Square in April.

1909   "Memoir of a Novelist" written.
        Virginia is left a legacy of £2,500 by Caroline Stephen in April.

1910   *Dreadnought* hoax in February.
        Virginia's health uncertain; rest cure prescribed from June–August.

1912   Leonard Woolf proposes in January.
        Virginia Stephen and Leonard Woolf marry in a civil ceremony in August.

Chronology

1913   Virginia unwell, under doctor's care in February.

1914   England enters WWI in August.

1915   Virginia's mental illness returns in February.
        The Voyage Out published in March.
        Virginia's health returns in November.

1917   Hogarth press publishes its first work, *The Mark on the Wall and Three Jews*, in July.

1919   *Kew Gardens* published by Hogarth Press in May.
        The Woolfs purchase Monk's House at auction in July.
        Night and Day published in October.

1920   "An Unwritten Novel" published in *London Mercury* in July.
        "Solid Objects" published in *Athenaeum* in October.

1921   *Monday or Tuesday* published in March.
        Virginia unwell from June–September.

1922   *Jacob's Room* published in October.

1923   "In the Orchard" published in *Criterion* in April.
        "Mrs. Dalloway in Bond Street" published in *Dial* in July.

1924   Virginia gives lectures resulting in "Mr. Bennett and Mrs. Brown" in May.

1925   *The Common Reader* published in April.
        Mrs. Dalloway published in May.

1927   "The New Dress" published in *Forum* in May.
        To the Lighthouse published in May.

1928   "Moments of Being: 'Slaters Pins Have No Points'" published in *Forum* in January.
        Virginia Woolf awarded *Femina Vie Heureuse* Prize in April.
        Orlando published in October.

1929   *A Room of One's Own* published in October.
        "The Lady in the Looking Glass: A Reflection" published in *Harper's Magazine* in December.

1931   *The Waves* published in October.

1932   *The Common Reader: Second Series* published in October.

1933   *Flush* published in October.

1936   Virginia finishes *The Years* and collapses of exhaustion in April.

1937   *The Years* published in March.

1938   "The Shooting Party" published in *Harper's Bazaar* in March.
"Lappin and Lapinova" published in *Harper's Bazaar* in April.
"The Duchess and the Jeweller" published in *Harper's Bazaar* in May.
Three Guineas published in June.

1939   Germany invades Poland; England enters WWII in September.

1940   *Roger Fry: A Biography* published in July.

1941   *Between the Acts* finished in February.
Virginia Woolf commits suicide in March.

Bibliography

Primary Works

Short Fiction

The Complete Shorter Fiction of Virginia Woolf, Edited by Susan Dick. New York: Harcourt, Brace, Jovanovich, 1985.

A Haunted House and Other Stories. Edited by Leonard Woolf. London: Hogarth Press, 1943; New York: Harcourt, Brace, 1944.

"The Journal of Mistress Joan Martyn." Edited by Susan Squier and Louis A. DeSalvo. *Twentieth Century Literature* 25 (1969):237–69.

The Mark on the Wall. London: Hogarth Press, 1917.

Monday or Tuesday. London: Hogarth Press, 1921; New York: Harcourt, Brace, 1921.

Mrs. Dalloway's Party: A Short Story Sequence. Edited by Stella McNichol. London: Hogarth Press, 1973; New York: Harcourt, Brace, Jovanovich, 1975.

Nurse Lugton's Golden Thimble. London: Hogarth Press, 1966.

Two Stories. With Leonard Woolf. London: Hogarth Press, 1917.

Autobiography and Criticism

Collected Essays. Edited by Leonard Woolf. 4 vols. London: Chatto & Windus, 1966–67; New York: Harcourt, Brace, & World, 1967.

The Diary of Virginia Woolf. Edited by Anne Olivier Bell. 5 vols. London: Hogarth Press, 1977–84; New York: Harcourt, Brace, Jovanovich, 1977–84.

The Letters of Virginia Woolf. Edited by Nigel Nicolson and Joanne Trautmann. 6 vols. London: Hogarth Press, 1975–80; New York: Harcourt, Brace, Jovanovich, 1975–80.

Secondary Works

Bibliographies

Majumdar, Robin. *Virginia Woolf: An Annotated Bibliography of Criticism, 1915–1974.* New York: Garland, 1976.

Bibliography

Rice, Thomas Jackson. *Virginia Woolf: A Guide to Research*. New York: Garland, 1984.

Books and Parts of Books

Bell, Quentin. *Virginia Woolf: A Biography*. 2 vols. New York: Harcourt, Brace, Jovanovich, 1972.

Daiches, David. *Virginia Woolf*. New York: New Directions, 1963.

DeSalvo, Louise A. "Shakespeare's *Other* Sister." In *New Feminist Essays on Virginia Woolf*, edited by Jane Marcus, 61–81. Lincoln: University of Nebraska Press, 1981.

Fleishman, Avrom. *Virginia Woolf: A Critical Reading*. Baltimore: Johns Hopkins University Press, 1975.

———. "Forms of the Woolfian Short Story." In *Virginia Woolf: Revaluation and Continuity*, edited by Ralph Freedman, 40–70. Berkeley: University of California Press, 1980.

Gordon, Lyndall. *Virginia Woolf: A Writer's Life*. New York: W. W. Norton, 1984.

Guiguet, Jean. *Virginia Woolf and Her Works*. Translated by Jean Stewart. London: Hogarth Press, 1965.

Holtby, Winifred. *Virginia Woolf*. London: Wishart, 1932.

Jackson, Gertrude. "Virginia Woolf's 'A Haunted House': Reality and 'Moment of Being' in Her 'Kew Gardens.'" In *Festschrift Prof. Dr. Herbert Kozoil*, edited by G. Bauer, F. K. Stanzel, and F. Zaic, 116–23. Vienna: Braumiller, 1973.

Majumdar, Robin, and McLaurin, Allen, eds. *Virginia Woolf: The Critical Heritage*. London: Routledge, 1975.

Mansfield, Katherine. "A Short Story: 'Kew Gardens' by Virginia Woolf," in *Novels and Novelists*, edited by John Middleton Murry, 36–38. New York: Knopf, 1930.

Rose, Phyllis. *Woman of Letters: A Life of Virginia Woolf*. New York: Oxford University Press, 1978.

Troy, William. "Virginia Woolf: The Poetic Method." In *Literary Opinion in America*, vol. 1, edited by Martin D. Zabel, 325–327. Gloucester, Mass.: Peter Smith, 1951.

Woolf, Leonard. *Beginning Again: An Autobiography of the Years 1911–1918*. New York: Harcourt, Brace & World, 1963.

———. *Downhill All the Way: An Autobiography of the Years 1919–1939*. New York: Harcourt, Brace & World, 1967.

Worrell, Elizabeth. "The Unspoken Word." In *Studies in Interpretation*, edited by Esther M. Doyle and Virginia H. Floyd, 191–203. Amsterdam: Rodopi, 1972.

Bibliography

Journal Articles

Araujo, Victor de. "'A Haunted House'—The Shattered Glass." *Studies in Short Fiction* 3 (1966)157–64.

Baldanza, Frank. "Clarissa Dalloway's Party Consciousness." *Modern Fiction Studies* 1 (1956):24–30.

Baldeshwiler, Eileen. "The Lyric Short Story: The Sketch of a History." *Studies in Short Fiction* 6 (1969):443–53.

Barzilai, Shuli. "Virginia Woolf's Pursuit of Truth: 'Monday or Tuesday,' 'Moments of Being' and 'The Lady in the Looking–Glass.' " *The Journal of Narrative Technique* 18 (Autumn 1988):199–210.

Bell, Clive. "Virginia Woolf." *Dial* (London), December 1924, 451–65.

Bishop, Edward L. "Pursuing 'It' Through 'Kew Gardens.'" *Studies in Short Fiction* 19 (1982):269–75.

Chapman, Robert T. "'The Lady in the Looking Glass': Modes of Perception in a Short Story by Virginia Woolf." *Modern Fiction Studies* 18 (1972):331–37.

———. "Parties . . . Parties . . . Parties: Some Images of the 'Gay Twenties.'" *English* (London) 21 (1972):93–97.

Dick, Susan. "'What Fools We Were': Virginia Woolf's 'A Society.'" *Twentieth Century Literature* 33 (1987):51–66.

Doner, Dean. "Virginia Woolf: The Service of Style." *Modern Fiction Studies* 2 (1956):1–12.

Fox, Stephen D. "'An Unwritten Novel' and a Hidden Protagonist." *Virginia Woolf Quarterly* 4 (1973):69–77.

Graham, J. W. "The Drafts of Virginia Woolf's 'The Searchlight.'" *Twentieth Century Literature* 22 (1976):379–93.

Hafley, James. "On One of Virginia Woolf's Short Stories." *Modern Fiction Studies* 11 (1956):12–16.

Hoffman, Charles C. "From Short Story to Novel: The Manuscript Revisions of Virginia Woolf's *Mrs. Dalloway*." *Modern Fiction Studies* 14 (1966):171–86.

Hungerford, Edward. "Is 'A Society' A Short Story?" *Virginia Woolf Miscellany* 21 (Fall 1983):3–4.

Latham, Jacqueline. "The Model for Clarissa Dalloway—Kitty Maxse." *Notes and Queries* (London) 16 (July 1969):262–63.

———. "The Origin of Mrs. Dalloway." *Notes and Queries* (London) 13 (March 1966):98–99.

Sakamoto, Tadanobu. "Virginia Woolf: 'Mrs. Dalloway in Bond Street' and *Mrs. Dalloway*." *Studies in English Literature* (Tokyo) 50 (1974):75–88.

Saunders, Judith P. "Mortal Stain: Literary Allusion and Female Sexuality in 'Mrs. Dalloway in Bond Street.'" *Studies in Short Fiction* 15 (1978):139–44.

Watson, Robert A. "'Solid Objects' as Allegory." *Virginia Woolf Miscellany* 16 (1981):3–4.

Reviews

Bennett, Joan. "Virginia Woolf." *New Statesman*, 26 February 1944, 144.

"Kew Gardens." *Times Literary Supplement*, 29 May 1919, 293.

MacCarthy, Desmond. "Authors and Their Fans." *Times* (London), 6 February 1944, 3.

Muir, Edwin. "New Short Stories." *Listener*, 2 March 1944, 250.

Strode, Hudson. "The Genius of Virginia Woolf." *New York Times Book Review*, 5 October 1941, 30.

"Virginia Woolf." *Times Literary Supplement*, 12 February 1944, 77.

Young, Marguerite. "Fictions Mystical and Epical." *Kenyon Review* 7 (1945):149–51.

Index

Index

Woolf, Leonard (husband), 13, 44–45, 50, 65, 72
Woolf, Mrs. (mother-in-law), 66
Woolf, Virginia, autobiography in fiction, 3, 6, 7–8, 19, 20, 27–28, 36–37, 39, 40, 44–45, 52–53, 55, 58, 64–67, 69–70, 72; characterization, 32–60; experimental writing, 5–6, *13–31*, 58–60; feminism, 7–8, 11–12, 35–36, 40, 70; finances, 4–5, 57, 61, 62, 68; ideas about history, 66, 72–73; ideas about reality, 13–15, 17, 99; marriage, 65, 66; political views, 44–45; reputation, 3–4, 73; social life, 7, 11, 36–37; style, 33, 41, 48, 62; traditional techniques, 4, 10, 61–73

WORKS—NONFICTION
Anon., 10
Common Reader, The, 57
Death of the Moth, The, 57
Flush, 57
"Modern Fiction," 5, 21, 32, 77–78, 109, 115
"Mr. Bennett and Mrs. Brown," 5, 32, 77–78
Room of One's Own, A, 10
Three Guineas, 10

WORKS—NOVELS
Between the Acts, 3, 115, 138
Jacob's Room, 3, 21, 72, 115
Mrs. Dalloway, 4, 33, 44, 50, 130–32, *134–38*
Night and Day, 21, 39, 110
Orlando, 61
To the Lighthouse, 4, 18, 43, 50, 72, 131, 133, 138
Voyage Out, The, 109, 129, 130
Waves, The, 4, 57, 138
Years, The, 4, 57, 58, 138

WORKS—SHORT STORIES
"Ancestors," *38–39*
"Blue and Green," 4, 24, 26

Complete Shorter Fiction of Virginia Woolf, The, 52, 106
"Duchess and the Jeweller, The," 4, 57, *61–62*, 68, 139
"Evening Party, The," 18, 29, 44
"Fascination of the Pool, The," 57, 58
"Gipsy, the Mongrel," 4, *68–70*
"Happiness," 38, 46
Haunted House, A, 67, 139
"Haunted House, A," 4, 23, 25, 105, *121–29*
"In the Orchard," 24, *26–27*
"Introduction, The," *39–41*, 42, 66
"Journal of Mistress Joan Martyn, The," *8–9*, 10, 11, 67, 68
"Kew Gardens," 4, *15–19*, 23, 24, 26, 57, 71, 105, *107–8*, *109–17*, 139
"Lady in the Looking Glass: A Reflection, The," 21, *55–57*, 77
"Lappin and Lapinova," 6, *64–67*, 139
"Legacy, The," 4, *70–71*, 72
"Lovers of Their Kind," 44; *See also* "Man Who Loved His Kind, The"
"Man Who Loved His Kind, The," *43–45*, 47, 130, 133–34
"Mark on the Wall, The," 4, *13–15*, 20, 21, 22, 24, 48, 57, 139
"Memoirs of a Novelist," *10–11*
"Miss Pryme," *58–59*
"Moments of Being: 'Slater's Pins Have No Points'," *52–55*, 77, *139–44*
Monday or Tuesday, 4
"Monday or Tuesday," 24, *25–26*
"Mrs. Dalloway in Bond Street," 4, 33
"Mysterious Case of Miss V., The," *8*, 10
"New Dress, The," *36–37*, 38, 40, 46, 47, 128, 131–32, 139
"Nurse Lugton's Curtain," *50–51*
"Ode Written Partly in

154

About the Author

Dean R. Baldwin is an associate professor of English at The Pennsylvania State University, Erie, The Behrend College, where he teaches the short story, composition, modern British fiction, and science and human values. His undergraduate degree in English and history was awarded by Capital University, and his M.A. and Ph.D. degrees are from Ohio State University. Originally trained as a medievalist, he has recently shifted his research interests to the modern British short story. His first book, a critical biography of H. E. Bates, was published by Susquehanna University Press. He has also contributed to Twayne's Critical History of the Short Story series and has published a book on V. S. Pritchett. In addition to teaching and writing, Baldwin is active in local and state professional organizations. His research in England and America has been supported by the Penn State Institute for the Arts and Humanistic Studies, the American Philosophical Society, and the National Endowment for the Humanities. He is currently working on a book about the economics of short story writing and publishing in Britain between the world wars.

About the Editor

General editor Gordon Weaver earned his B.A. in English at the University of Wisconsin-Milwaukee in 1961; his M.A. in English at the University of Illinois, where he studied as a Woodrow Wilson Fellow, in 1962; and his Ph.D. in English and creative writing at the University of Denver in 1970. He is the author of several novels, including *Count a Lonely Cadence, Give Him a Stone, Circling Byzantium,* and most recently *The Eight Corners of the World* (Vermont: Chelsea Green Publishing Company, 1988). Many of his numerous short stories are collected in *The Entombed Man of Thule, Such Waltzing Was Not Easy, Getting Serious, Morality Play,* and *A World Quite Round.* Recognition of his fiction includes the St. Lawrence Award for Fiction (1973), two National Endowment for the Arts fellowships (1974, 1989), and the O. Henry First Prize (1979). He edited *The American Short Story, 1945–1980: A Critical History.* He is a professor of English at Oklahoma State University and serves as an adjunct member of the faculty of the Vermont College Master of Fine Arts Writing Program. Married, and the father of three daughters, he lives in Stillwater, Oklahoma.